Archaeological Excavations in the Greek Islands

Archaeological Excavations
in the Greek Islands

by
DOROTHY LEEKLEY
ROBERT NOYES

NOYES PRESS
PARK RIDGE, NEW JERSEY

Published in the United States by
NOYES PRESS
Noyes Building
Park Ridge, New Jersey 07656

Leekley, Dorothy.
    Archaeological excavations in the Greek islands.

    Bibliography: p.
    Includes index.
    1. Islands of the Aegean—Antiquities. 2. Ionian
Islands—Antiquities. 3. Excavations (Archaeology)—
Islands of the Aegean. 4. Excavations (Archaeology)—
Greece—Ionian Islands.
I. Noyes, Robert, joint author. II. Title.
DF895.L43   939.1   75-34931
ISBN 0-8155-5043-X

FOREWORD

This book describes archaeological excavations undertaken in the Greek islands. It is the first of a series of three books which will relate to archaeological excavations in all of Greece. The two forthcoming volumes to be published in 1976 are entitled, "Archaeological Excavations in Southern Greece," and "Archaeological Excavations in Central and Northern Greece."

The information given for each site in each of these volumes will include the names of excavators, the dates in which the excavations were carried out, a very brief description of the finds, and, most important, a bibliography which will enable the researcher to locate the book and/or article which describes in greater detail the excavations and finds in which he is interested. Reports of travelers and secondary literature are for the most part not included in this book.

Maps of the archaeological sites will not be included here. Current Greek maps are a hazardous trap for the unwary, and the authors have found that the drawing of maps and the precise locating of all these excavations on the maps are tasks which would require so much time as to delay the publication of the first three volumes. Plans to publish a fourth volume consisting solely of maps of the Greek archaeological sites are under way.

One of the reasons for publishing these books is to correct the present difficulty which exists in obtaining information on minor archaeological sites. Information on major excavations is simple enough to locate; consequently entries on such sites as Delos or Knossos are very brief. This book will contain information on all excavated sites in the Greek islands, many of which can be considered as minor. For the most part, entries have been limited to sites at which planned excavations have taken place. Chance finds and rescue operations, except for the most important, have been excluded. These finds have been reported, for Crete, in *Cretika Chronika,* and since 1960, for all of Greece in *Archaeologikon Deltion.* Sites on which ancient remains have been noted, but not excavated, have also generally been omitted. Sites dating from all periods up to the Roman have been included, except for early Christian remains.

The information in this book is as current as possible up to the mid-1970's. However, it must be realized that many excavations of the Greek

Archaeological Service are not reported for a few years after the work has been done. Those who use this book should utilize it in conjunction with the invaluable *Archaeological Reports* issued annually by the Council of the Society for the Promotion of Hellenic Studies and the Managing Committee of the British School at Athens as a supplement to *Journal of Hellenic Studies*, and the annual report published in *Bulletin de Correspondance Hellénique* issued by École française d'Athénes.

In every book of this nature, a question arises regarding the difficult task of transliterating Greek into English. The authors have used a "mixed" system, conforming to no particular rules, but attempting to choose the most commonly accepted spelling; historic spellings are used for the better known sites. The material presented in this book was taken from numerous periodicals in many languages, and no attempt has been made to transliterate any specific name on a consistent basis.

This book is organized by island groupings, and with the exception of Crete, Greek political subdivisions are ignored. Crete, because of its size, has been organized by its four political subdivisions (nomes).

Miss Dorothy Leekley received her B.A. in Classics from Queens University, Kingston, Ontario, and is presently a doctoral student in Greek at Bedford College, University of London, working specifically on religion in Phyrgia in the Greek and Roman periods. Robert Noyes is a publisher of books relating to archaeology, classics and ancient history. He has been to Greece a number of times to visit sites, and is particularly interested in the relationship of Greek geography and prehistory.

CONTENTS

East Central Crete–Nomos Irakliou

Ionian Islands

ANTIKYTHERA: Excavations were made by Stais for the Greek government (*AD* 1889, 171). He discovered the base of a statue and a temple of Apollo Aegileus. The major site on the island is at Palaiokastro with quite significant walling for such a small island. Sherds found on the island date from the 5th century BC to the 1st century AD. Additional information is given by R. Leonhard (*Die Insel Kythera*, Gotha 1899) and R. Hope Simpson (*BSA* 56, 1961).

An important shipwreck was found off the northern coast in 1900 and was reported by Kavvadias (*JHS* 21, 1901, 205ff); quantities of statuettes, bronzes, pottery, glass, etc. were recovered. G. Weinberg re-examined the finds in the 1960's and fixed the date of the shipwreck as 80–50 BC, but the source of the cargo was not determined (*Trans. Am. Philos. Soc.* 55, pt.3). An important sophisticated gearing mechanism was found and discussed by D. Price (*Gears from the Greeks*, N.Y. 1975).

ARKOUDI AND ATOKOS: Miss Sylvia Benton made a few comments on these two small islands (*BSA* 32, 1931–32, 232), after a trip in 1925. On Arkoudi, she simplified Dörpfeld's findings (*Alt-Ithaka* 1927, 98ff) by reporting a large wall between the two highest summits. On Atokos, she found Hellenistic pottery and a Byzantine coin.

CORFU: Most of the late 19th and early 20th century exploratory work on the Island of Corfu was related to the attempt to prove that Corfu was the land of Scheria, from which the Phaeacians sailed with Odysseus to deposit him on Ithaca. Schliemann (*Ithaka, der Peloponnes und Troja*, Leipzig, 1869) in 1867 thought that the capital of the Phaeacians was on the Palai-

1

opolis peninsula just south of Corfu town. Bérard in 1901 believed (on literary and topographical evidence) that Paleokastritsa in the northwest was a likelier site (_Nausicaa et le retour d' Ulysse,_ vol. 4 of _Les Navigations d' Ulysse,_ 1927), and Dörpfeld explored this and other areas in the northwestern part of the island. However, nothing has ever been found that relates Corfu to the Odyssey. In fact (with few exceptions), the only prehistoric sherds found on the island have been Neolithic or earlier. All other finds are eighth century BC or later, verifying the statement of Thucydides and Strabo that Corfu was colonized from Corinth in 734 BC.

Essentially all of the intensive excavations conducted on Corfu have been on the Palaiopolis peninsula, south of modern Corfu town. This was the site of the original Corinthian settlement, and was always the most important settlement on the island. There have also been scattered excavations in the northern, northeastern, and northwestern portions of the island.

In 1822, Colonel Whitmore was digging for a spring in the Analipsis and 'Mon Repos' areas south of Corfu town and uncovered ancient ruins of a temple. In 1843, the Lion of Menakrates (620–550 BC) was discovered in the same area at Garitsa.

The first important excavations on the island were undertaken beginning in 1910 by the Ephors Versakis and Rhomaios, and the German Institute directed by W. Dörpfeld with the support of Kaiser Wilhelm II. South of Corfu town, near the Ayi Theodori Convent, an Archaic Doric temple, shown to be a temple of Artemis, was excavated. The sculpture on the west pediment, with the running Gorgon, was almost completely preserved, and is one of the finest examples of Greek Archaic sculpture yet found.

Work continued on this temple through 1914, and Rhomais carried out supplementary work in 1919–20. Short reports were published at the time (_PAE_ 1911, 164ff) (_AA_ 1911, 135ff; 1912, 247ff; 1913, 105ff; 1914, 46ff) (_AM_ 39, 1914, 161ff), and the final publication appeared much later (Archäologisches Institut des Deutschen Reiches, _Korkyra, archaische Bauten und Bildwerke,_ Band I: H. Schleif, K. Rhomaios et al., _Der Artemistempel,_ Berlin 1940; Band II: G. Rodenwalt, _Die Bildwerke,_ Berlin 1939).

In 1911 Dörpfeld conducted trials in other parts of Corfu and he again uncovered the Archaic temple discovered by Whitmore at 'Mon Repos' (short report, _Korkyra,_ Band I, 143ff) (_AM_ 39, 1914, 170ff). In the same year he and Rhomais discovered a prehistoric settlement in the northwest at Cape Kephali, and claimed the finding of monochrome sherds with a small admixture of sherds of Mycenaean technique (_AR_ 1912–13, 367ff).

In 1939, Papademetriou excavated at Roda, on the north coast, where he discovered a Doric temple of mid-fifth century BC (_PAE_ 1939, 85ff). Further clearing was done by 1968 and the finds reported (_AD_ 21, 1966, _Chr._ 2, 329) (_AD_ 22, 1967, _Chr._ 2, 367ff).

Between 1954 and 1961, V. Kallipolitis conducted excavations at the Palaiopolis Church (Ayia Kerkira) south of Corfu town, which was damaged during World War II. He found several occupation levels in the area, but nothing earlier than proto-Corinthian; and it appears that the earliest Corinthian settlement of the island was located here between the two harbors. Finds included fragments from an early 5th century Doric temple, and assembly area, and material through Roman times, including Roman baths. Kallipolitis also explored the northern part of the island in 1957 and 1961, finding fragments from a fifth century Doric temple at Ayia Agathi, near Avliotes; traces of a Hellenistic stoa near Karousadhes; a stone axe near Spartilla; and bronze statuettes near Dhafni (*PAE* 1955–59) (*Ergon* 1961).

In 1958 Kallipolitis began a thorough reinvestigation of the 'Mon Repos' temple site, and G.S. Dontas, beginning in 1962, carried out most of the excavation. There was a large Archaic temple (identified as a Heraion), the finds indicating that the site of the temple was a sanctuary at the beginning of the Corinthian colonization. A Classical temple was later built there. P. Kalligas was also involved in the excavations. The finds have been reported as follows: (*Kathimerini* Jan. 17, 1965) (*AR* 1965–6, 14) (*AD* 19, 1964, *Chr.* 3, 315ff; 20, 1965, *Chr.* 2, 378ff; 21, 1966. *Chr.* 2, 317ff; 22, 1968, *Chr.* 2, 360ff) (*AAA* 1, 1968, 66ff) (*AR* 1968–69, 22) (*AD* 23, 1969, *Chr.* 2, 303ff).

Dontas also excavated at Kanoni, at the southern end of the Palaiopolis peninsula, in a residential area, formerly a cemetery (*AD* 20 *Chr.*). Under the late fifth and third century houses, sub-Geometric and proto-Geometric pottery were found.

In 1971 a Roman building complex was found at Kassiopi, in the northeastern part of the island by K. Kostoglou-Despini (*AAA* 4, 1971, 2, 202ff).

In addition to the prehistoric sites mentioned here, others include Sidari, Gardiki, Vatos, and a cave on Mount Ayios Mathaios. The prehistory of the island has been a specialty of Professor Sordinas. There is a report of his surface survey of prehistoric sites in 1965 (*Kerkyraika Chronika* 11, 1965, 141ff). Dontas also has prepared a summary of Sordinas' prehistoric investigations with a map indicating the finding of prehistoric sherds (*AD* 21, *Chr.* 2, 326ff). On the island generally, see the book by Raymond Matton (*Corfou*, Athens 1960).

ITHACA: Explorations and excavations of the island of Ithaca have always been romantically intertwined with the desire to find the palace of Odysseus and the other locations mentioned in the Odyssey.

In 1806, W. Gell explored the island and conducted some minor excavations on the summit of Aetos (*Geography and Antiquities of Ithaca*, 1807). Leake visited the island at about the same time and undertook some cursory digging at Aetos (*Travels in Northern Crete*, 1835). There is also another report (*Archaeologyia* 33, 1849). During two visits in 1868 and 1878, Schliemann dug trial trenches on Aetos, hoping to find the palace of Odysseus, not realizing that the acropolis was too high in elevation for a Mycenaean palace. He also dug trenches at Polis, Ayios Athanasios, at the cave of Dexia, and at Marathia (*Ithaca, der Peloponnes, und Troja*, 1869; *Ilios*, 1880).

In 1896 Dörpfeld and Wilhelm explored the island; and with Goekoop and Preuner in 1900, Dörpfeld made perfunctory excavations at Pelikata, Polis, Kastro Malos, and Ayios Athanasios. At about this time Dörpfeld became convinced that Leukas was the original Ithaca of the Odyssey, and this theory is developed in detail in his book (*Alt-Ithaka*, Munich 1927). The opposing view that modern Ithaca is the Homeric Ithaca was postulated by Victor Bérard (*Ithaca et la Grèce des Achéens*, 1927). Also see W. Vollgraff ("Dulichion-Leukas," *Jahrbuch*, 1907, 617).

In 1904, Vollgraff conducted extensive investigations, in the plain of Vathy, the cave of Marmaraspelia, at Aetos, Pelikata, Ayios Athanasias, and the spring of Melanudros. The sherds found by Vollgraff (*BCH* 1905, 145ff) were important clues for the BSA expedition in the early 1930's under the direction of W.A. Heurtley, assisted by S. Benton, C.R. Watson, T.C. Skeat, and T. Emmett. The BSA expedition was sponsored by a Homeric scholar, Lord Rennel of Rodd, who was also of the opinion that modern Ithaca was Homeric Ithaca (*BSA* 33, 1ff) (*Homer's Ithaca*, 1927), and was disturbed by the Dörpfeld theory that Homeric Ithaca was modern Leukas.

The results of these important excavations have been reported in the following articles: W.A. Heurtley and H.L. Lorimer, "LH III–Proto-Geometric Cairns at Aetos," (*BSA* 33, 1932–33, 22ff); Heurtley, "The Early Helladic Settlement at Pelikata," (*BSA* 35, 1934–35, 1ff); S. Benton, "The Cave at Polis I," (*BSA* 35, 1934–35, 45ff) and "The Cave at Polis II," (*BSA* 39, 1938–39, 1ff); Heurtley, "Excavations in Ithaca, 1930–35, Summary of the Work," (*BSA* 40, 1939–40, 1ff); Heurtley and M. Robertson, "Excavations in Ithaca V—The Geometric and Later Finds from Aetos," (*BSA* 43, 1948); Benton, "Second Thoughts on Mycenaean Pottery in Ithaca," (*BSA* 44, 1949, 307ff); H. Waterhouse, "Excavations at Stravros, Ithaca in 1937," (*BSA* 47, 1952, 227ff); Benton, "Further Excavations at Aetos," (*BSA* 48, 1953, 255ff); and Benton and Waterhouse, "Excavations in Ithaca: Tris Langadas," (*BSA* 68, 1973, 1ff).

There appears to have been continuous habitation in Ithaca from the Early Bronze Age down to Roman times. On Aetos there is no evidence of prehistoric habitation but sherds from LH IIIC to Roman times were found. At Pelikata, primarily EH sherds were found with very minor amounts of Minyan and LH III. Very few Mycenaean sherds were found in nearby Ayios Athanasios and Asprosykia. Mycenaean sherds were found at Tris Langadas, with remains of rectangular and apsidal buildings. At the cave of Polis a stratified deposit of votive offering, tripod-cauldrons, and pottery from Bronze Age through Roman times were uncovered.

Other articles of interest include: S. Benton, "A Votive Offering to Odysseus," (*Antiquity* 10, 1936, 350); S.E. Bassett, "The Palace of Odysseus," (*AJA* 23, 1919, 288ff); a summary is given by Wace and Stubbings (*A Companion to Homer*, 1962); and there are additional comments in a book by Desborough (*The Last Mycenaeans and Their Successors*, 1964).

The 'Ithaca Question' has never been resolved, but it appears to be more likely that Homeric Ithaca is modern Ithaca, rather than modern Leukas. The most logical result of fitting the literary, topographical, and archaeological evidence together results in locating Arethusa's Fountain, the plain of Marathia (for the stable of Eumaeus), and the Korax, in the southeastern part of the south island; the landing place of Telemachus upon returning from Pylos and Sparta, at Ayios Andreas Bay in the southernmost part of the south island. Dexia Bay would be the landing place at Odysseus. The 'Cave of the Nymphs' is located a mile or so south of Dexia Bay, and it is somewhat too far distant to fit in with the description of the Odyssey. In 1806 Gell had found another cave right at Dexia Bay, now lost, which would tie in better with the literary evidence.

In the northern part of the island, candidates for the Palace of Odysseus are Pelikata, Ayios Athanasios, or Tris Langadas. Pelikata appears to be the more obvious choice for the palace of Odysseus, since it commands a good view of all three bays (Frikes, Afales, and Polis) and the surrounding seas, which would eminently suit this piratical gentleman. The village of Stavros may have been the settlement below the palace, and the farm of Laertes could have been somewhere in the area near Pelikata.

KALAMOS: Sylvia Benton explored the island in 1925, giving particular emphasis to a fort of polygonal masonry on the northeastern end of the island. She is of the opinion that a large settlement existed nearby at Episkopi, which was littered with sherds, had remains of fortification walls, and houses of polygonal masonry. She also visited the villages at Kalamos, Kephali, and Kastos (*BSA* 32, 1931–32, 233ff).

KEPHALLENIA: Apparently, the first excavations on this island were conducted by the collector Major De Bassett (*RA* 37, 128ff; and *Catalogue*

Musée d'Histoire, Neuchatel, Switzerland). Between 1883 and 1915, a number of excavations were undertaken at various locations by Kavvadias, Kyparissis, Philadelpheus, and Marinatos. The results of these excavations were reported in Greek archaeological publications and S. Benton has prepared a table indicating the sites, dates, excavators and bibliographical references (*BSA* 32, 1931–2, 228). Many of these excavations were sponsored and financed by A.E.H. Goekoop, a wealthy Dutchman, who was of the opinion that Homeric Ithaca, Dulichion, and Same, were different areas of Kephallenia. After his death, his widow supported further excavations by Marinatos, a native Kephallenian, who was destined to become head of the Greek Archaeological Service. The later work of Marinatos was reported (*AE* 1932 and 1933). Other information is found in the following articles: (*PAE* 1951, 185ff) (*AJA* 36, 1932, 61) (*AA* 1932, 148) (*AR* 1931–2, 247-8).

The sites excavated prior to World War II included those in the area south and southeast of Argostoli (Mazarakata, Kokkolota, Kangkalisais, Lakkethra, Diakata, Kranea, Gephyra, Metaxata); Oikapeda in the northwest; the area south of Phiskardo in the northeast; at Kakolangada in the center between Argostoli and Same; Korneli in the southeast, and Same in the east. Kranea was a major occupation site at one time. The walls at Same of Hellensitic date also indicate a large settlement.

After World War II, Kallipolitis excavated a Roman villa in 1957 near Skala (*BCH* 82, 1958, 727ff) (*AD* 17, 1961–2, *Mel.* 1ff). Marinatos excavated in the area in 1960, finding the foundations of an Archaic temple and Mycenaean chamber tombs (*Ethnos,* 23, Dec. 1960).

In the Same area, Kallipolitis excavated three 4th century tombs in 1958 (*BCH* 83, 1959, 658ff). He also explored the Roman baths north of Same in 1959 (*BCH* 84, 1960, 729ff) and continued his investigation in 1960.

In 1968, P. Kalligas investigated the remains on the two hills of the acropolis of Kranea, and found a prehistoric deposit containing handmade Bronze Age pottery; he describes the classical and Roman remains. At Pronnos in the southern part of the island, prehistoric sherds were found as well as three late Archaic tombstones. He also describes other remains in the island, particularly the Skala site first investigated by Marinatos (*AD* 24, *Chr.* 2, 1969, 270ff).

Most of the information regarding prehistoric habitation on the island comes from tombs and very little from settlements. The preponderance of LH IIIC pottery found in conjunction with local handmade pottery could indicate flight from the mainland due to the disturbances at the end of LH IIIB (Desborough, *The Last Mycenaeans and Their Successors*). S. Benton reported on her survey of the island (*BSA* 32, 1931–2, 220ff).

KYTHERA: In the 19th century, Schliemann thought he had located the ancient temple of Aphrodite. Stais excavated a chamber tomb at Lioni, about one km north of Khora (*AD* 1, 1915, 191ff). Benton discovered a prehistoric settlement on the headland of Kastri, beside the bay of Avlemon on the coast facing Crete (*BSA* 32, 1931–2) in which MM to LM II pottery had been used.

R. Hope Simpson carried out a short survey in 1957 and 1958, in two periods of about a week each, and summarized his findings (*BSA* 56, 1961, 148ff). Sites visited by him include Pyreatides, Vithoulas, Lioni, cave of Ayia Sophia, Kastri, Palaiopolis, Palaiokastro, Elleniko and Mitata. EH sherds and obsidian were found in the north of the island. MM II through LM II sherds were found at Kastri and other locations. LH III sherds were found, probably indicating Mycenaean dominance and Cretan decline.

In 1963 the British School undertook a trial excavation (*AR* 1963–4, 25) at Kastri, followed by two five-week seasons of selective excavation in 1964 and 1965. Work on the material found in the Minoan settlement was conducted in 1966, and study of the tomb material in 1967. The report published (*Kythera* 1972, Noyes Press, USA) was chiefly concerned with discoveries made in the Minoan colony at Kastri; however, antiquities of earlier and later periods are also discussed. Authors include J.N. Coldstream, G.L. Huxley, R. Hope Simpson, J.F. Lazenby, A.S. Trik, B. Anderson, W.G. Forrest, J. Herrin, A.H.S. Megaw, and W.H. Plommer.

The finds made at Kastri extend in time from the Early Bronze Age until the middle Byzantine period, with most abundant finds from MM III and LM I. The Minoans were aware of the value of Kythera as a stepping stone on the route from Crete to the Peloponnese. The Minoan colony was abandoned and reoccupied by Mycenaeans in LH IIIA2. The authors agreed with the identification of Kastri (or Palaiopolis) with Homeric and Classical Skandeia. Older accounts of Kythera include those by Leonhard (*Die Insel Kythera*, 1899), Reimann (*Recherches Archéologiques sur les Iles Ioniennes*, 1879) and Weil (*AM* 1880, 224ff).

LEUKAS: The most important explorer and excavator on Leukas was Wilhelm Dörpfeld, who was of the opinion that Homeric Ithaca was modern Leukas. He also identified Homeric Same with modern Ithaca, and Homeric Dulichion with modern Kephallenia. In an attempt to prove his point he conducted extensive excavations in the first decade of the 20th century, and continued to explore the island until his death. His work has been summarized (*Alt-Ithaka*, Munich 1927). He had some financial support from A.E.H. Goekoop.

Dörpfeld believed that the palace and town of Odysseus were located in or near the plain of Nidri, northwest of Vlicho Bay. He found the remains of a few buildings in the plain, and a number of grave circles. Neolithic, EH and MH Minyan sherds were discovered. Very little Mycenaean was found, which was disappointing to the followers of Dörpfeld's theory. S. Benton believes that Dörpfeld underestimated the amount of Neolithic pottery, and erred in other identifications (*BSA* 32, 1931–2, 230). Further exploration and excavation may yet uncover Mycenaean habitation, since the island of Meganisi just off-shore was found to contain large numbers of LH sherds.

V. Kallipolitis and P. Kalligas also excavated on the island. In the 1960's, trials in caves near Fryni, west of Leukas town, resulted in finds from prehistoric through Hellenistic times (*AD* 23, 1968, *Chr.* 2, 321ff; 24, 1969, *Chr.* 2, 277ff). Today a large body of scholarly opinion believes that modern Leukas was Homeric Dulichion.

MEGANISI: Sylvia Benton visited the island in 1925. She explored a cave below the village of Spartochori, finding Neolithic or Early Bronze Age sherds, Hellenistic terracotta plaques, and a Roman flagon. South of the village of Spartochori there were several fields covered with Late Bronze Age sherds. She also explored the extensive ruins at Limena Batheos, which includes a Classical foundation; a seventh century sherd was found (*BSA* 32, 1931–2, 230ff). These Mycenaean finds, according to S. Benton and R. Hope Simpson, on an island so close to Leukas, signify further potential Mycenaean finds on Leukas.

ZAKYNTHOS: Nineteenth century explorers of Zakynthos include O. Riemann (*Recherches Archéologiques sur les Iles Ioniennes,* 1879) and B. Schmidt (*Die Insel Zakynthos,* 1899). In 1925 and 1926, Sylvia Benton visited the island and recorded her observations (*BSA* 32, 1931–2, 213ff).

In 1934, Miss Benton and Miss Lorimer excavated at Akroterion and Kalogeros (*AA* 1934, 161). At Akroterion (near Halikais) a Mycenaean tholos tomb and settlement were excavated. In this area, a well on the property of Eleos was found, containing LH IIIA–B pottery. At Kalogeros (near Vasiliko) a settlement was excavated, producing LH IIIA–B sherds, Geometric figurines, and Archaic terracottas. Miss Benton feels that the Hellenic town of Zakynthos was on the site of Castle Hill in the capitol city of Zante. The Italians dug in Zakynthos during World War II, but no reports are available. Miss P. Agallopoulou reported Mycenaean cist tombs at Kambi containing LH IIIC1 vases (*AAA* 5, 1972, 63ff).

Argo-Saronic Islands

AEGINA: At the site of the Late Archaic temple of Aphaia in the northeast of the island, the architect C.R. Cockerell conducted a short and superficial excavation in 1811, and removed what sculptures were found. The sculptures went eventually to the Glyptothek in Munich. The results of his work were published much later (Cockerell, *The Temples of Jupiter Panhellenius at Aegina*, etc., London 1860) (Inscriptions: *JHS* 6, 1885, 143ff; 340ff; sketches: *JHS* 29, 1909, 53ff).

B. Stais conducted a short excavation in 1894 (*PAE* 1894, 20ff) and in 1901 Adolf Furtwängler, with Herrmann, Thiersch and Fiechter excavated the site more thoroughly. An inscription proved that the temple was dedicated to the local goddess Aphaia, not to Zeus Panhellenius as Cockerell had thought. In addition to finding some other pieces of sculpture, fragments of an earlier 6th century Doric temple, a great altar, and subsidiary buildings were discovered. Bronze and terracotta votives of the Geometric period, Mycenaean, Geometric, proto-Corinthian, Corinthian and Naucratite vases were found, and a series of Mycenaean terracotta figurines, many near the cave below the temple terrace. A preliminary report was published, (*Sitzungber. d. Bayer, Akad.* 1901, 363ff) and then a final report by Furtwängler, Thiersch, and Fiechter (*Aegina, das Heiligtum der Aphaia,* 2 vols., Munich 1906) (cf. G. Welter, *Aigina*, Berlin 1938, 64ff).

In 1951–53 Orlandos undertook to renovate and restore the temple, and in 1966–69 D. Ohly, sponsored by the German Institute, explored north and east of the temple, including the slopes outside the temenos, and found Archaic fragments. He thoroughly investigated the retaining walls to determine the location and orientation of the earlier temple (*AA* 1966, 515ff; 1970, 48ff; 1971, 505ff).

In 1901 and the following years before his death in 1907, Furtwängler and his colleagues excavated a small shrine on the torrent at Trypiti, northeast of the temple of Aphaia. The shrine is probably a Nymphaion,

9

and probably Hellenistic, though there are older remains nearby (Furt-wängler, *Aegina,* plates 12.1; 16.4) (*AA* 1938, 518ff).

The same year they excavated briefly at Palaiochora, the capital of the island from the 8th century AD and at the Sanctuary of Zeus Hellanios on 'Oros' or Ayios Ilias, the highest peak on the island. Work was occasionally done on these sites during the 1920's and 1930's. On Oros there was a Late Bronze Age settlement, abandoned at the end of the Mycenaean era. The site was reoccupied in the Geometric period, and the sanctuary reached its height in the Hellenistic period, when the whole mountain was sacred to Zeus, worshipped as the rain-bearer. There are remains of Hellenistic buildings on a terrace (but not of a temple) and on the peak itself is an altar (*AA* 1938, 101ff) (G. Welter, op. cit. 26ff, 91-92) (Furtwäng-ler, *Aegina,* 73ff) (Ålin, 1962, 114ff).

Modern Aegina town occupies part of the ancient city. The Kollona hill, on the promontory north of the town, with a temple of Apollo (c. 520–500, once believed to have been dedicated to Aphrodite) was the ancient citadel, occupied since Neolithic times. In 1894 B. Stais excavated on the east slopes of the hill by the temple, and found prehistoric houses with Mycenaean vases (*AE* 1895, 235ff). The vases were reported by L. Pallat (*AM* 22, 1897, 265ff). Thiersch, in conjunction with Furtwängler's excavation of the temple of Aphaia, dug briefly in 1901. In 1904, Keramo-poullis excavated Mycenaean tombs in the vicinity (*AE* 1910, 177ff).

Paul Wolters conducted major excavations at Kollona from 1924 to 1926; the work was continued through 1931 by G. Welter, and again during the war (*Gnomon* 1925, 46ff) (*AA* 1925, 1ff; 1937, 19ff). Debris from an earlier temple was found, and an important fortified prehistoric settlement. The EH settlement was to the west of the temple. An EH smelting furnace was found, and Cycladic stone vases and pottery. The MH site extended to the area later occupied by the temple. Matt-painted, Minyan and imported wares of EM III–MM III were found. The LH settlement, extending through Mycenaean times, was built on the ruins of the MH settlement (Welter, *Aigina,* Berlin 1938). Work was resumed again in 1966 under Hans Walter (Salzburg), with particular emphasis on the EH fortifications, and continued through 1972, when houses of the Neolithic period were found. There is also a Mycenaean cemetery and an enormous cemetery dating from the late Geometric times to the 6th century. This consists largely of cist graves cut in the rock, and a type of chamber tomb peculiar to Aegina. The final reports of Walter's excavation have begun to appear with: W.W. Wurster (*Alt-Ägina,* vol. I.1, Mainz, 1974).

On the westernmost point of the island Welter investigated a grave mound 16 m in diameter. He suggests that this is the monument of the Aeginetans who fell at Salamis.

Kallipolitis has reported an Archaic chamber tomb (6th century) with six sarcophagi near the old Kapodistria orphanage (*AD* 19, 1964, *Chr.* 74ff).

HYDRA: In September 1975, a team led by Peter Throckmorton, technical advisor to the Hellenic Institute of Marine Archaeology, discovered an early Bronze Age shipwreck near the islands of Hydra and Dhokos, with pottery which dates the wreckage to about 2500 BC, thus making it the oldest shipwreck discovered to date.

POROS: The ruins of ancient Kalauria lie on the Palatia plateau. In 1894 S. Wide and L. Kjellberg of the Swedish School excavated there. Little was revealed except the plan of the foundations of the Doric temple of Poseidon and nearby buildings. The sanctuary dates from the 6th century, though use of the site goes back to Early Helladic and Mycenaean times. Close by are the remains of the city's agora and a heroon (*AM* 20, 1895, 267ff) (cf. G. Welter, *Troizen und Kalaureia*, Berlin, 1941).

SALAMIS: In 1893 Kavvadias excavated a necropolis of more than 100 tombs near the arsenal. This important cemetery was the first find of a large number of sub-Mycenaean graves. The finds have been discussed by S. Wide (*AM* 35, 1910, 17ff) and C.-G. Styrenius (*Op. Ath.* 4, 1962, 103ff). The graves cannot be dated accurately within the sub-Mycenaean/ proto-Geometric period because, despite the large number of vases, the tombs themselves were not well reported at their discovery (cf. Styrenius, *Submycenaean Studies*, Lund, 1967).

In 1915, Phourikos excavated an LH grave in modern Salamis Town (*AE* 1916, 8) (cf. *AE* 1948–49, 114).

In 1958 W. McLeod explored the site of the Athenian fort of Boudoron in the northwest of the island opposite the Megarid (*Hesperia* 29, 1960, 316ff).

In 1961 Miss A. Andriomenou excavated a Mycenaean chamber tomb at Limnionas between Ambelakia and Silenia, and a sub-Mycenaean tholos tomb at Kamini near Ambelakia (*AD* 17, 1962, *Chr.* 39). In 1964 C. Davaras excavated nine chamber tombs near the gymnasium containing Myc. IIIA to IIIC vases (*AD* 20, *Chr.*) (*AR* 1964–5, 6).

Northern Aegean Islands

LEMNOS: In the Neolithic period Lemnos had the most advanced civilization known in the Aegean. Transition from the Bronze Age into the Geometric period continued without any sharp break, and though Hellenized from the 8th century, Lemnos was probably not populated by Greeks until the 6th century.

Nineteenth century explorers of the island included Conze in 1858 (*Reise auf den Inseln des Thr. Meeres,* Hannover 1860, 104ff). Cousin and Durrbach noted inscriptions including the non-Greek inscription from Kaminia (*BCH* 10, 1886, 1ff) and Picard and Reinach found more inscriptions and numerous tombs (*BCH* 36, 1912, 326ff).

C. Fredrich explored the island in 1904. He worked particularly at Myrina, excavating a cemetery which contained 7th century and possibly earlier graves with handmade pottery. He also excavated the Kastro at Myrina, finding walls, house remains, and the foundation of a temple. He also noted rock graves at Kaminia, prehistoric walls on the small acropolis of Exo-Kastro near Kaminia and the remains of a temple of Heracles at Komi (*AM* 31, 1906, 60ff; 241ff). F.L.W. Sealy surveyed the island, noting among other things that little was left of Fredrich's temple at Komi (*BSA* 23, 1918–19, 148ff).

Professor Allesandro Della Seta of the Italian School began excavations in 1926 at Kokkino (Palaiopolis) on the bay of Pournia in the north of the island, the site of Classical Hephaistia. He continued each season through 1930, and again in 1937–39. This was the principal city of Lemnos in Classical times, but the settlement goes back at least to the sub-Mycenaean period. Classical remains include a 5th or early 4th century theatre, succeeded by a Roman theatre. Of the pre-Greek period, there are houses, a sanctuary, possibly dating from the ninth century and continuing in use until the end of the 6th century, and cemeteries of the 9th-8th centuries (*Ann.* 8-9, 1925–26, 393; 10-12, 1927–29, 711ff) (C. Anti, *Atti del' Instituto Ven. di Scienze, Lettere ed Arti,* 89, 1929–30, 733ff) (D. Mustilli, "La necropoli tirrenica di Efestia," *Ann.* 15-16, 1932–3, 1ff).

In 1937–39 Della Seta excavated on the other side of the harbor, at Chloi, the site of a sanctuary of the Kabeiroi. Remains of Hellenistic and Roman buildings overlay pre-Greek material, including foundations of an Anaktorion, a Telesterion and a stoa (*Ann.* 17-18, 1939–40, 223ff; 19-21, 1941–3, 75ff) (Doro Levi, "Il Cabirio di Lemno," *Demosieuma tès en Athenais Archaiologikes Etaireias* 3, 1964; *Charisterion eis A.K. Orlandos;* 110ff).

Between 1931 and 1936, Della Seta and others excavated the Neolithic and Early Bronze Age settlement at Poliochni, on the northeast coast below Cape Voroskopos about 3 km from Kaminia. Poliochni had a highly developed Neolithic culture which considerably antedates Troy I. Neolithic fortification walls and towers, in some places 5 m high, stone baths and cement cisterns were found in the second Neolithic city. Earthquakes were the cause of successive destructions. The site was unoccupied during Troy III and IV periods, and then an unfortified settlement was built corresponding to Troy V. Only one sherd suggests any later occupation. The Poliochni Bronze Age culture had close connections with Troy and Lesbos, but Cycladic and Greek mainland material attest wider associations (L. Bernabò-Brea, *Poliochni*, Rome 1964).

In 1962 S. Kharitonides reported finding terracottas of the 5th to 3rd century BC at Myrina (*AD* 18, 1963, *Chr.* 265). In 1960 the reef off the east coast, called 'Ifaloi Keros', was explored by underwater techniques, and marble from an Archaic temple of Apollo was discovered; this was supposed to be the city of Chryse, which according to Herodotus was engulfed by an earthquake.

SAMOTHRACE: Archaeological excavations have been conducted for over a hundred years at the site of the Sanctuary of the Great Gods, located in the north of the island at Palaiopolis. To the east of the sanctuary are the remains of the ancient city.

In 1863 Champoiseau, the French Consul at Adrianopolis, discovered the Nike now in the Louvre. In 1866 G. Deville and E. Coquart partially excavated the site and published a short report (Deville, *Archives des missions scientifiques* 4, 253ff).

In 1873 and 1875 two Austrian expeditions under Alexander Conze, with Hauser, Niemann and Benndorf, dug at Samothrace, excavating the Arsinoeion, a round building, built c. 285 BC, the Hieron, a temenos, the monumental gateway to the site known as the Ptolemaion, the Nike bastion, a stoa, and the walls and a tower of the town fortifications (A. Conze et al., *Archaeologische Untersuchungen auf Samothrake*, Vienna 1875–80). In 1891 Champoiseau returned and discovered a theatre. In 1923–27 an expedition under the auspices of the French School, directed by Salac and Chapouthier, excavated at the site (*BCH* 51, 1927–8, 353ff, on city walls; *BCH* 80, 1956, 118ff, on the theatre).

Beginning in 1938 intensive explorations were begun by the Institute of Fine Arts of New York University under Karl Lehmann. They commenced again after the war in 1948, and have continued yearly to the present. Karl Lehmann died in 1960, and his wife Phyllis Lehmann was appointed acting director. Others involved have included J.R. McCredie, E. Dusenberg and A. Vavritsas. Reports were originally published in *AIA* 43, 1939, 133ff; 44, 1940, 485ff), but since 1950 have been in *Hesperia* (*Hesperia* 19, 1950, 1ff; 20, 1951, 1ff; 21, 1952, 19ff; 22, 1953, 1ff) and volumes of the final publications have appeared beginning in 1958 (*Samothrace, Excavations Conducted by the Institute of Fine Arts of New York University*, The Bollinger Foundation, N.Y.).

In addition to work on previously discovered buildings, these excavations have included the Anaktorion, a 5th century building for preliminary initiation which replaced a still earlier building, an altar court, and cemeteries. Samothrace was not colonized by Greeks until c. 700, and it is clear that the sanctuary is much older and that some elements of pre-Greek usages survived into later times. Inscriptions in a non-Greek language were found on votive vases (*Hesperia* 24, 1955, 93ff). Underneath the Arsinoeion was found a 7th century precinct enclosing a much earlier rock altar associated with a Cyclopean retaining wall in whose fill prehistoric sherds were found. The Altar Court also had been built over a rock outcrop which had been cut to serve as an altar.

Elsewhere in the island, Vavritsas located an EB Age settlement at Kariotis, a few miles east of the ancient town, in 1955.

THASOS: Considerable excavation has been undertaken on the island, mostly on the site of the ancient city of Thasos, located on the north coast at the modern capital, Limen, or Thasos. Conze visited the island in 1858 and particularly noted the fortified towers throughout the island (Conze, *Reise auf den Inseln des Thr. Meeres,* Hannover, 1860). In 1886 in Thasos town Bent noted a Roman arch, sculpture, inscribed pedestals, and graves south of the city walls (*Classical Review* 1, 1887, 210ff).

In 1910 the French School began a series of major excavations at the ancient city, which, with interruptions by the two World Wars, continues to this day. The excavation was initally directed by Adolphe Reinach. Thasos was only colonized by Parians about 700 bc and so most of the finds date from the Archaic period at earliest, but use of the site continued through Byzantine times and to the present. The site is quite large and includes the port area, residential quarters, the lower town with an agora, Odeion, and a number of sanctuaries, and the acropolis above. The fortification walls are particularly extensive; almost the entire circuit can be traced, with towers, gates, and a 6th century secret stairway. The walls date from about 412 BC but were built on earlier foundations. An interesting find in 1960 was an apsidal building with Early Iron Age pottery of Macedonian-Thracian type, indicating settlement prior to the Parian colonization, and in 1961 soundings revealed traces of 8th century occupation. One difficulty in discovering pre-Parian remains is that the high water level in the lower town prevents examination of the underlying levels.

French activities are reported yearly in *BCH*. More complete reports have been published by L'École française d'Athènes in a series entitled *Études Thasiennes*, beginning in 1944. Also available is the *Guide de Thasos*, 1967. Excavators have included Bon, Seyrig, Devambez, Launay, Avezou, Martin, Treheux, Roux, Salviat, Dunant, Weill, Bernard, Servais, Rolley, Regnot, Picard, Garlan, Maffre, Holzmann, Grandjean, and Knoepfler.

Notes on the topography of the entire island were made by C. Fredrich (*AM* 33, 1908, 215ff), Baker-Penroyre and Tod (*JHS* 29, 1909, 91ff, 203ff), and A. Bon (*BCH* 54, 1930, 147ff). Of the other sites on the island, one of the more important is a sanctuary at Aliki on the southeastern coast. It was explored by Bent in 1886 (*JHS* 8, 1887, 434) and in 1924 and 1961–62 by the French School. The sanctuary includes two temples; the form apparently dates from the Archaic period (*BCH* 1962, 949ff) (*AD* 17, 1961–2, *Chr.* 251ff). In 1962 Miss A. Romiopoulou excavated a nearby cave containing votive pottery and figurines dating back to the late 7th century (*AD* 18, 1963, *Chr.* 257ff).

Another site is at Theologos, the medieval capital of the island. There is a probably Hellenistic tower here and in 1925 the French School excavated a necropolis with grave reliefs (*BCH* 49, 1925, 465). A prehistoric settlement was located on the Kastri hill near Theologos in 1969. There is what is perhaps a prehistoric citadel wall, and LN, EB and Early Iron Age sherds were found. On a neighboring hill, at Kentria, Late Bronze Age and Early Iron Age cist tombs were found (*AD* 25, 1970, *Chr.* 2, 401). In the same year another prehistoric settlement was located in a cave near Maries in the south (*AD* 25, 1970, *Chr.* 2, 400). LN and EB sherds were found (*AAA* 3, 1970, 215ff).

There are Hellenistic towers or forts at many other places, including st' Aulakia and Gravoussa on Potamia Bay, at Helleniko, and in the south near Astris (*BCH* 54, 1930, 147ff).

Northern Sporades

HALONNISOS: In 1969, Theochares reported the discovery of Middle Palaeolithic stones associated with fossilized animal bones at Kokkino-kastro (*AD* 25, 1970, *Chr.* 2, 276ff). Similar deposits have been found further north at Glipa and Steni Vala.

KYRA PANAYIA: In 1969, Theochares made a trial excavation within a Neolithic settlement on the islet of Ayios Petros, in a bay on the southwest side of the island. There were two levels of EN occupation, and a third belonging to the transition period between EN and MN (*AD* 25, 1970, *Chr.* 2, 271ff).

SKIATHOS: C. Fredrich (*AM* 31, 1906, 99ff) and A.J.B. Wace (*AM* 31, 1906, 129ff) reported on the island, mostly on the medieval remains.

SKOPELOS: C. Fredrich (*AM* 31, 1906, 99ff) and A.J.B. Wace (*AM* 31, 1906, 129ff) have reported on Skopelos. Platon has excavated a Mycenaean tomb at Staphyles (*BCH* 62, 1938, 481).

SKYROS: In 1893 Max Mayer excavated what he called 'pre-Attic' tombs on the island (*BCH* 17, 1893, 207-8). C. Fredrich surveyed the island (*AM* 31, 1906, 257ff), and worked particularly at the acropolis above the modern town. He also noted a temple at Cape Markesi in the north.

The area of Skyros town has been occupied since Neolithic times. In 1918 Evangelides found Bronze Age sherds near Skyros town and excavated Geometric graves (*AD* 4, 1918, *par.* 34ff). In 1935 Papademetriou investigated an extensive necropolis north of the town on the northwest bank of the river, and dug rich sub-Mycenaean—proto-Geometric graves (*AA* 1936, 228ff), and Stravropoullos found similar graves along the shore in 1938 (*AJA* 43, 1939, 131). In 1945 Theochares found more than 100 Neolithic sherds on the cliff east of the city (*AE* 1945–7 *Chr.* 1ff).

In 1958 Theochares found what may be Paleolithic implements in a cave by the Bay of Akhili on the east coast, 5 km south of Skyros town. He also excavated a Neolithic settlement at Papa to Khoma by the shore, east of the acropolis (*Kathimerini* March 2, 1958).

A survey of the island has been prepared by H.D. Hansen ("Prehistoric Skyros," *Studies Presented to David M. Robinson*, vol. I, St. Louis 1951, 54ff).

Eastern Off-Shore Islands

CHIOS: Modern Chios town is the site of the ancient city. The earliest serious excavations were those of Fustel de Coulanges in 1845. He excavated on the south slope of the Palaiokastro hill in the modern town and found an ancient wall (*Archives des missions scientifiques* 5, 1856, 492ff). Since then, not only the wall, but the hill itself has disappeared (*BSA* 49, 1954, 124). Kourouniotes excavated thirty late 6th century burials on the Latomi hill in the town (*AD* 1, 1915, 64ff; *AD* 2, 1916, 190ff). Kondoleon reported an Archaic cemetery in the southwest area of the town, which he excavated in 1952–53 (*PAE* 1952, 520ff; 1953, 268ff). In 1952 M.S.F. Hood and J.K. Anderson excavated the Kofina ridge on what would have been the north edge of the ancient town, uncovering nineteen late Hellenistic tombs and traces of occupation back to Archaic time (*BSA* 49, 1954, 123ff). In 1953 Stephanos found a 3rd century BC inscription which has some variation in detail from the Homeric Catalogue of Ships, and a votive deposit of a Demeter sanctuary of Hellenistic and earlier times (*AR* 1953, 162). A summary of what is known of ancient Chios town is given by Boardman (*BSA* 49, 1954, 123ff).

The temple of Apollo Phanaios at Kato Phano, the ancient Phanai, on the southwest coast, was discovered and partly excavated by Kourouniotes in 1913–15 (*AD* 1, 1915, 64ff; *AD* 2, 1916, 190). Winifred Lamb of the British School with Miss Six and Mr. Brock conducted further excavation in 1934. The site was inhabited from the 9th century. There are Geometric and Archaic walls, and sherds of all periods from Geometric through Classical. The temple, of which only the foundations remain, and an enclosure wall, date probably from the 6th century (*BSA* 35, 1934–5, 138ff).

In a survey of the island, J.M. Cook noted tombs and house remains in the water at Kato Varvasi, which is possibly the site of ancient Leuconium. At Daskalopetro on the north outskirts of Chios town he noted that what is traditionally called the School of Homer is probably an Archaic sanctuary of Rhea or Cybele (*BSA* 41, 1940–45, 33ff).

In 1937 and 1938 Miss Eccles and Miss Jeffrey excavated the Ayios Galas cave. Material dates from all periods from Neolithic through Roman. Neolithic pottery, flint, bone and obsidian were found. The Neolithic material had affinities with Lemnos, Thessaly and Macedonia, and the Bronze Age finds with Anatolia (*AR* 1938–9, 203).

Beginning in 1952 and through 1955 a prehistoric settlement was excavated by M.S.F. Hood and J. Boardman on a hill on the southeast coast at Emporio. A fortified Early Bronze Age settlement, continuing into the Middle and Late Bronze Age, was located. A late Roman fortress was built on top of the hill. On Mount Profitis Elias above Emporio an Archaic town was explored. Dr. and Mrs. Ventris surveyed the site. A temple of Athena with votive deposits dating back to the early 8th century was found, and houses were excavated on the slopes. The town took form about 700 BC and seems to have been abandoned by 600, though a new temple was built in the mid 6th century, which continued in use until the Hellenistic period. Later occupation, probably a 5th–3rd century farm house and a late Roman construction, were discovered in 1954 at Pindakas about 2 km inland (*BSA* 53-4, 1958–59, 295ff).The area by the harbor with the early Christian basilica was also investigated. The basilica overlay a late Archaic temple, and a votive deposit perhaps belonging to an earlier temple was discovered. A report of the excavations on Mt. Profitis Elias and in the harbor sanctuary was published (John Boardman, *Excavation in Chios 1952–1955: Greek Emporio. BSA* suppl. no. 6, 1967). A final report is being prepared by Sinclair Hood.

At Nagos in the northeast of the island Evangelides excavated an ancient building (*PAE* 1921, 45ff) and Stephanos found part of a kouros figure there in 1961. In 1954 Hood and Boardman conducted trials in the Athenian naval base at Delphinion on the northeast coast and cleared part of the defense wall and a nearby Hellenistic farmhouse (*BSA* 51, 1956, 41ff).

Also in conjuction with the Emporio excavations an underwater reconnaissance was made of the south and east coasts and many ancient wrecks were identified (R. Garnett and J. Boardman, *BSA* 56, 1961, 104ff).

IKARIA: L. Politis excavated three sites on the island in 1938 and 1939. At Kampos (ancient Oinoe) he found only a poor fifth century grave, and a sarcophagus of the third century AD. In 1969, N. Zafeiropoulos discovered a small Roman Odeon-like building at Kampos (*AD* 25, 1970, *Chr.* 2, 421ff). At Rakhes, graves of a poor fifth to third century cemetery were dug. At Nao, on the northwest of the island, various fragments (including those of a temple) were found as well as numerous sherds from many periods (*PAE* 1939, 124ff).

In 1955, N. Kondoleon discovered an acropolis going back to Archaic times at Therma (ancient Thermi), near Kataphiyon. Classical and later tombs were found along the road leading north to Kataphiyon.

LESBOS (MYTILENE): C.T. Newton lived on Lesbos and reported on various antiquities (*Travels and Discoveries in the Levant*, London 1865). R. Koldewey excavated at Klomidados, hoping to locate the temple of Apollo Napaios, but was not successful. He also explored other parts of the island (Koldewey, *Die antike Baureste der Insel Lesbos*, 1890). In 1921, 1927 and 1928 Evangelides excavated at Klopede in Kalloni, about 5 km west of Ayia Paraskevi, finding two temples, one of which is believed to be that of Apollo Napaios. The capitals and columns were of Aeolic type; a Geometric fibula was also found. Trial excavations were again conducted in 1972, with much Geometric and Early Archaic Lesbian bucchero ware found (*AAA* 1972, 39ff).

A two-week trial excavation at Methymna, the island's second largest city, was conducted by Winifred Lamb in 1928, north of the town. Occupation went back to the 7th century, and possibly to the 9th, and extended to Roman times. Excavation was not continued as the soil is shallow and considerably disturbed.

Between 1929 and 1933 Miss Lamb excavated the prehistoric site of Thermi, about eight miles north of Mytilene. Five occupation levels were discovered at the site. It was first occupied in the early third millenium, and depopulated about 2000 BC, with much of the pottery having affinities with Trojan ware. The site was reoccupied during Mycenaean times, and destroyed possibly a hundred years later. Nothing on the site seems later than Troy VIIA (W. Lamb, *Excavations at Thermi in Lesbos*, Cambridge, 1936).

Miss Lamb also excavated at Antissa, in the western part of the island, in 1931 and the following years. The settlement on the promontory was occupied from Mycenaean times. One of the more interesting finds was an apsidal building of the 10th or 9th century, which was succeeded by another apsidal building in the 8th century; both were probably temples. There was a good deposit of Lesbian bucchero ware on the site (*BSA* 31, 1930–1, 146ff; *BSA* 32, 1931–2, 41ff).

Various excavations have been conducted in the area of the capital, Mytilene. In 1958 Evangelides excavated the well-known theatre northwest of the town (*PAE* 1958, 233ff). In 1961 Kharitonides excavated a section of a defense wall (400 BC), and exposed a late Roman house (*AD* 17, 1961–2, 261ff). In 1961–63 he excavated at Khorafa, and uncovered interesting mosaics of the 3rd–4th century AD which illustrate scenes from Menander's comedies. They have been published by Kharitonides, Kahil and Ginouvès (*Antike Kunst*, 6th Beiheft, 1970). Additional mosaics were found by B. Petrakos near the church of Ayios Therapon in 1970 (*AD* 24, 1969, *Chr.* 368ff).

In 1967 Petrakos cleared the Ionic temple at Mesa, originally excavated by Koldewey in the 1880's (*Ergon* 1967, 72ff; 1968, 68ff).

In 1949, J.M. Cook explored the island and found prehistoric sites at several locations, the most extensive being north of Perama on the west shore of the Gulf of Iera. In 1962 Christomanos directed underwater searches at Kourtir, the landing stage of Lisvori on the Gulf of Kalloni, which may have been the ancient Pyrra, mentioned by Pliny (NH V 139), as well as the location of the Lesbians' joint sanctuary of Zeus, Hera, and Dionysos (*Kathimerini* Dec. 23, 1962). Kharitonides noted a prehistoric settlement on the Khalakies promontory in 1960 (*Kathimerini* Dec. 18, 1960).

PSARA: In 1961, S. Kharitonides explored the island. Just south of the modern town on the Palaiokastro promontory he located a considerable settlement from Late Geometric to Late Classical or Hellenistic times. On the west coast on the shore of the Bay of Arkhontiki, he discovered Mycenaean cist graves; with sherds assigned to Myc. IIIB (*AR* 1961–2, 23) (*BCH* 86, 1962, 878) (*AD* 17, 1961–2, *Chr.* 266).

SAMOS: The site of the Heraion on the south coast was visited by the Society of Dilettanti in 1812 and by Ross in 1841 (*Reisen* 2, 1843, 142ff). Some excavation was carried out by Gerard in 1879 (*BCH* 4, 1880, 383ff) and Clerc in 1883 (*BCH* 9, 1885, 505ff), and by Kavvadias and Sophulis (*PAE* 1902, 11ff; 1903, 10ff). Large excavations were undertaken by the German Institute with T. Wiegand, M. Schede and von Gerkan in 1910–1914 (Wiegand, "Erster vorläufiger Bericht," *Deutsche Akademie der Wissenschaften*, formerly Königliche or Preussische Akademie . . ., *Abhandlungen, philosophisch-historische Klasse*, 1911, 1ff; M. Schede, "Zweiter vorläufiger Bericht," op.cit., 1929, 1ff). A second series of excavations was begun by Buschor in 1925 and continued to 1939. Others taking part included Welter and Reuther. Among the more important publications (*AA* 1929, 147ff) (*AM* 55, 1930, 1ff) (*AM* 58, 1933, 1ff, the entire issue devoted to the Heraion). After World War II repair work was done; excavation was resumed in 1953 and has continued since.

Other directors included U. Jantzen, H. Walter, and W. Martini. A series of final publications began to appear in 1961. The site of the Heraion goes back to the Bronze Age, and immediately east and north of the temple a prehistoric settlement was found (V. Milojcic, *Samos I: Die prähistorische Siedlung unter dem Heraion*, Bonn 1961). The Heraion reached its greatest development in Archaic times under Polycrates and was utilized continuously through the Roman period (cf. Oscar Reuther, *Der Heratempel von Samos*, Berlin 1957).

Excavations have also been conducted at the site of ancient Samos at Tigani, renamed Pithagorio. Guérin described the ancient remains (*Description de l' île de Patmos et de l' île de Samos*, Paris, 1856, 192ff). Fabricius excavated in the city, particularly the tunnelled aqueduct which goes more than 1000 feet through a mountain, built by Eupalinos for Polycrates c. 524 BC. It is described by Herodotus (III 60) as one of the greatest works in Greece (*AM* 9, 1884, 163ff). Buschor and Wrede of the German Institute excavated in 1928 and 1930, uncovering a Roman villa at the Castle of Logothetes, and discovering Neolithic sherds. Janzten and others resumed excavation in 1965; they confirmed the Neolithic occupation level, and uncovered other levels through Roman times. A palatial Hellenistic building was identified. The Hellenistic walls were built over Archaic and Classical courses. The city reached its peak as capital of the island under Polycrates in the 6th century BC. In 1968 Jantzen studied the plan of the ancient harbor, the basin of the modern harbor being half the size of the ancient one (*AA* 1928, 623ff; 1931, 268ff) (*AM* 54, 1929, 110ff; *AM* 60-1, 1935–1936, 112ff on prehistoric finds) (*AA* 1969, 101ff, 435ff; 1971, 221ff and annually since). A guide to the ancient city and the excavations was published by R. Tölle (*Die Antike Stadt Samos*, Mainz 1969). In 1969, C. Tsakos reported the discovery of a large quantity of sixth century pottery, with Attic black-figure being particularly abundant.

Other finds included the location by Yialouris in 1955 of a 4th century BC building at Kedro, 6 km from Limin Vatheos, fragments throughout the plain of Misokambos, Roman material at Samiopoulos, and Archaic material from Mitilinioni (*AR* 1955, 26-7). In 1961 Zafeiropoulos found a Mycenaean chamber tomb near Miloi (*BCH* 1961, 839) (*AR* 1961–2, 23).

The Dodecanese

Books and articles covering more than individual islands include:

1. Ludwig Ross, *Reisen auf den griechischen Inseln,* 3 vols., Stuttgart 1840–45.
2. G. Gerola, *Ann.* 2, 1916, 1ff.
3. R.N. Dawkins and A.J.B. Wace, *BSA* 12, 1905–6, 15ff.
4. P.M. Fraser and G.E. Bean, *The Rhodian Peraea and Islands,* Oxford 1954, mostly historical rather than archeological.
5. G.E. Bean and J.M. Cook, *BSA* 52, 1957, 116ff.
6. G. Susini, *Ann.* 41-42, 1963–64, 203ff.
7. R. Hope Simpson and J.F. Lazenby, particularly for the Bronze Age:
   "Notes from the Dodecanese," *BSA* 57, 1962, 154-175.
   "Notes from the Dodecanese II," *BSA* 65, 1970, 47-77.
   "Notes from the Dodecanese III," *BSA* 68, 1973, 127-179.
   (These are abbreviated henceforth as *Dod.* 1, *Dod.*2, and *Dod.* 3.)

The Dodecanese were not formally annexed to Greece until 1948. They were occupied by Italy from 1912 to 1945, and much of the archaeological work in the Dodecanese has been done by Italians. There are many sites included in this survey, however, which have often been visited and described, but never excavated. Outside of Kos and Rhodes, there has been relatively little in the way of major excavations in recent years.

ALIMNIA: The only known ancient site on this small island off the west coast of Rhodes is a fortified Hellenistic tower, 4th–3rd century BC. It is reported by Gerola (*Ann.* 2, 1916, 11) and Susini (*Ann.* 41-2, 1963–4, 260ff).

ASTYPALAIA: The ancient remains have been treated by Dawkins and

Wace (*BSA* 12, 1905–6, 151ff), Gerola (*Ann.* 2, 1916, 70ff) and Hope Simpson and Lazenby (*Dod.* 3, 157ff).

The Kastro of the modern Khora town is the site of the ancient acropolis and the Venetian castle. Little that is ancient remains—some walls, probably Hellenistic—but numerous sherds attest to continuous occupation from Late Geometric through Hellenistic times. This is the chief ancient site on the island.

At the Moura spring south of Khora, prehistoric sherds, either Late Neolithic or Early Bronze Age, and Roman sherds were noted (*Dod.* 3, 16).

The Kastro of Ayiou Ioannou, overlooking the west coast, is another medieval fort on an ancient site. Obsidian, Early Bronze, and Mycenaean sherds, a possibly prehistoric wall foundation, as well as Classical sherds were noted in 1970 (*Dod.* 3, 162ff).

In 1970 Miss I. Zervoudakis and Miss A. Archontidou excavated a Mycenaean chamber tomb at Patelles near Armenochori (*Dod.* 3, 161), and G. Konstantinopoulos reports two more Mycenaean chamber tombs on the island (*AAA* 6, 1973, 120).

In 1970 Richard Hope Simpson surveyed the island and located numerous Late Chalcolithic or EB I sites of Cycladic type. Besides Kastro Ayiou Ioannou they include: a hill southwest of Ayios Nikolaos chapel on Panormos Bay, Kastro Vayi in the north of the central isthmus, Helleniko on Vathy Bay (also a Hellenistic refuge tower), and two sites on Agrelidhi Bay in the southeast. Mycenaean finds are scanty in comparison (*Dod.* 3, 159ff).

CASTELLORIZO: The Palaiokastro hill was described by Kyparissis (*AD* 1, 1915, *Par.* 62ff). The site was apparently occupied from the 5th or 4th century onwards, though the preserved fortifications are probably Hellenistic. The site is largely built over with medieval remains (cf. *Dod.* 2, 73). Kyparrisis noted Cyclopean walls on the summit of Vigla (op.cit., 63) but they could not be seen in 1967 (*Dod.* 2, 75).

The most prominent feature of the harbor town of Castellorizo is the 'Red Castle' of the Knights of St. John, from which the island takes its name. The site had previously been occupied by a Classical fort, but there are no remains. In the cliffs below the Castle is a rock-cut tomb similar to ancient tombs on the Lycian mainland opposite. It is described and planned by Hope Simpson (*Dod.* 2, 76-7), who suggests that it may date from the late fifth or early fourth century.

CHALKI: This island has been described by Gerola (*Ann.* 2, 1916, 6ff),

Susini (*Ann.* 41-2, 1963–4, 247ff) and Hope Simpson and Lazenby (*Dod.* 3, 156-7). The Kastro of the modern Khorio, with the medieval castle of the Knights of St. John, was the ancient acropolis, and there are traces of ancient fortifications. In 1931 the Italians under Jacopi excavated a necropolis of rich Classical tombs on the north side of Potamo Bay to the east of Khorio (*Clara Rhodos* 2, 1932, 117ff), and other burials are known in the area.

KALYMNOS: The chief surveys of Kalymnos are those of Bean and Cook (*BSA* 52, 1957, 127ff) and Hope Simpson and Lazenby (*Dod.* 1, 172ff). The two areas in which ancient sites are found are Pothia town and the valley behind it, and the Vathy area in the east above the small harbor of Rina.

In 1854–55 Newton excavated in the area called 'Damos' on the road running northwest from Pothia to Sykia, approximately at the watershed (Charles Thomas Newton, *Travels and Discoveries in the Levant I*, London 1865, 283ff). Near the Ierosalem Chapel he excavated the temple of Apollo which was the Kalymnians' depository in the 4th century, but an Archaic marble head and Archaic and Classical sherds were also found at the site. There are also remains of a theatre. The temple was re-examined by the Italians under Segre in 1937–39 (*Memorie dell' Istituto storico-arch. di Rodi* 3, 1938, 33ff). Newton also excavated Hellenistic tombs and a settlement site, relocated by Hope Simpson and Lazenby on a tongue of land between two ravines opposite the Arkangelos Church about 1 km past the Ierosalem Chapel (*Dod.* 1, 173). Newton had noted house foundations and an extensive stretch of fortification wall with a tower, but in 1960 Hope Simpson and Lazenby found the site denuded, though they noted blocks built into field walls and found black-glazed and Hellenistic sherds.

There was an important Mycenaean and later settlement on the Perakastro hill above Pothia. There is a medieval fort, but Myc. IIIA and IIIB sherds were found in abundance (*Dod.* 1, 172). On the opposite side of the valley Neolithic and Mycenaean pottery was found in the Ayia Varvara cave in 1920 and in another nearby cave in 1921 by the Italians (*Clara Rhodos* 1, 1928, 106ff). Paton excavated a series of Mycenaean tombs dug into the pumice on the banks of the torrent by Perakastro hill. The vases were dated as Myc. III B-C (*JHS* 8, 1887, 446ff) (cf. *Dod.* 1, 172ff).

In the Vathy area, the Italians found Neolithic, Kamares, and Late Mycenaean sherds in the Daskalio cave above Rina in 1922 (*Clara Rhodos* 1, 110ff) (cf. *BSA* 52, 1957, 128). Mycenaean sherds have also been noted near the Hellenistic tower at Phylakai (*BSA* 52, 1957, 128). At Embolas, near Metokhi village abour 4 km inland from Rina, a site was noted by Newton (op.cit., 319ff) and Ross (*Reisen* 2, 112). There are remains of an ancient circuit wall, and blocks and architectural pieces are built into local chapels and houses. Fourth century and Hellenistic sherds were noted, and there are Roman tombs scattered throughout the valley (*BSA* 52, 1957, 128ff) (*Dod.* 1, 172-3).

One publication (*Ann.* 22-3, 1944–5) is entirely devoted to the history and topography of Kalymnos.

KARPATHOS: On Karpathos generally, see R.M. Dawkins (*BSA* 9, 1902–3, 176ff), Fraser and Bean (*The Rhodian Peraea and Islands*), Susini (*Ann.* 41-2, 1963–4, 57ff), and Hope Simpson and Lazenby (*Dod.* 1, 159ff, and *Dod.* 2, 68ff). The island has also been visited by Ross (*Reisen* 3, 1845, 56ff) and Bent (*JHS* 6, 1885, 23ff). On the question of whether there was an ancient city named Karpathos on the island, see Dawkins (op.cit., 204), Fraser and Bean (op.cit., 141-2 and notes), and (*Dod.* 1, 159, note 34).

The Acropolis above Pigadhia on the east is possibly the ancient Potidaion. There are remains of ancient circuit walls (Ross, op.cit.) (Dawkins, *BSA* 9, 203) and sherds from Classical and later periods, perhaps going back to the Archaic period, were found in abundance on the top and south slopes. In 1960 Hope Simpson and Lazenby were unable to find any clear evidence of Mycenaean habitation on the site, but in view of the typically Mycenaean nature of the rocky citadel and the closeness of Mycenaean graves, they feel that this was also the Mycenaean fortress (*Dod.* 1, 159-60). A Mycenaean chamber tomb was discovered about 400 m south of the harbor on the outskirts of Pigadhia in the late 1950's. A few bronze weapons and about 90 vases were recovered. About half were either Minoan or imitative of MM IIIB or LM IA. The others are Myc. IIIA with a few IIIB (Kharitonides, *AD*, 17, 1961–2, *Mel.*, 32ff). On the western outskirts of Pigadhia next to the guest house there is evidence of a LH IIIA and IIIB settlement, perhaps going back to MM IIIB or earlier (*Dod.* 1, 160-1, *Dod.* 2, 68-9). Bent records obtaining a stone female idol from Pigadhia town (*JHS* 6, 1885, 233ff).

The ancient city of Brykous on the northwest has been described by Bent (op.cit., 236ff), Dawkins (op.cit., 204) and Della Seta (*Boll.d'Arte, ser.* II, 4, 1924–5, 85ff). There are remains of late Classical or Hellenistic city walls and in 1884–5 Bent excavated rock-cut tombs of Classical and later periods. Hope Simpson and Lazenby noted "possibly" Mycenaean pottery (*Dod.* 1, 161-2).

Ancient Arkaseia in the southwest was visited by Ross (op.cit.) and Dawkins (op.cit., 201ff). There are extensive remains of walls, though they have been used as a quarry since Ross's day. There is an abundance of Classical and later sherds, and Hope Simpson and Lazenby found obsidian flakes and some possibly Mycenaean sherds (*Dod.* 1, 162-3).

Northwest of Pigadhia is an area with considerable ancient remains, around the villages of Aperi, Voladha, the Palaia Pi spring, and Lastos. The Kastro hill at Aperi, described by Susini (*Ann.* 41-2, 225ff) has a medieval fort on the summit, but 5th–4th century and later sherds were found on the slopes. Geometric tombs are reported and later tombs are known (*AA* 1932, 182). At Pini near Voladha there are sporadic traces of habitation, mostly Hellenistic and Roman. An inscription was found here, referring to the 'koinon of the Eteokarpathians' and mentioning a temple of Apollo at Karpathos (*IG* xiii. 1, 977). Near the Palaia Pi spring northeast of Voladha is a small acropolis which overlooks the east shore of Karpathos. Fourth century and Hellenistic sherds were found. At Lastos, northwest of Palaia Pi, is a steep hill with remains of walls and cisterns, Hellenistic and perhaps earlier. Hope Simpson and Lazenby suggest that this whole area may have formed a 'koinon' and the Kastro at Aperi, which would dominate Pigadhia Bay and yet be secure, may have been more important than the harbor town until the Classical period (*Dod.* 1, 165).

Mycenaean vases and a bronze sword were reported by W.R. Paton from a tomb in the Yiafani area in the northeast (*JHS* 8, 1887, 449). The exact site is unknown, but it is suggested (*Dod.* 1, 161) that it may have come from the terraced area known as Kambi to the south.

Other ancient remains on the island are mostly Hellenistic or Roman, and include a series of forts in the west central area (*Dod.* 1, 165-6).

KASOS: The island is described by Ross (*Reisen* 3, 1845, 32ff), Susini (*Ann.* 41-2, 1963–4, 20ff), and Hope Simpson and Lazenby (*Dod.* 1, 168; *Dod.* 2, 69ff). The main ancient center was the Kastro at Polin. There are remains of ancient terraces and house walls. Ross saw a relief of a youth and a hare, now in the museum at Pigadhia on Karpathos. There are numerous Classical and Hellenistic sherds, and Bronze Age and Geometric sherds were noted (*Dod.* 2, 70). Emborio was probably the ancient harbor, though the only remains noted were Roman (ibid., 80).

Susini (op.cit., 206ff) explored the Ellinokamara cave and reported sherds of various periods including MM and Mycenaean. There is a Hellenistic blocking wall in the entrance (*Dod.* 2, 71-2).

At Ellinika Grammata in the northeast there is a sanctuary with an inscription to the Nymphs (Susini, op.cit., 213ff) (*IG* xii, 1, 1042).

KOS: The modern town of Kos is the site of the ancient Kos, or Kos Meropis, but the capital of the island was only moved here in 366 BC, and since then it has been destroyed several times by earthquakes. A small mound in the modern town known as the Seraglio was excavated by the Italians in 1936, 1940–43, 1946, and since. This was found to be part of a Geometric necropolis with cist and pithoi burials, mostly babies and children. It was discovered that these tombs were sunk into a Bronze Age settlement. Pottery from this settlement included MM III, LM IA and IB, and Myc. III A–B (*Ann.* 43-4, 1965–6, 306) (Morricone, *Boll. d'Arte*, 35, 1950, 316ff). Kondis made some new soundings on the site in 1959 (*Ergon* 1959, 131ff).

In 1935 and 1940–41 Morricone excavated two large Mycenaean cemeteries at Langadha and Eleona southwest of Kos city, less than 1 km from the Seraglio settlement. The graves are chamber tombs or caves cut in the pumice, and the pottery is Myc. IIIA1–IIIC2 (*Ann.* 43-4, 1965–6, 5ff). In 1900 Herzog excavated an Archaic fountain sanctuary dedicated to Demeter, with vases and terracottas of the late 6th or early 5th century (*AA* 1901, 134ff). The Italians with L. Laurenzi excavated the city during their occupation; finds included Classical burials and reliefs, a Roman theatre, baths, an Odeion, three temples to Aphrodite, Pontia and Heracles by the harbor (*Clara Rhodos* 1, 98ff; 9, 73ff). Compared to the apparent importance of the area in the Mycenaean period, there is relatively little evidence of the period from Late Geometric to Hellenistic times, during which the old capital, Astypalaia, perhaps the Dorian foundation, was the more important city.

In 1898 Herzog searched for the site of the famous Koan sanctuary of Asclepius. He was unsuccessful, but published over 200 inscriptions, about half from Kos city (R. Herzog, *Koische Forschungen und Funde*, Leipzig, 1899). He did later discover the Asklepieion and excavated there from 1900. The site consists of three great terraces, with a number of temples. The temple of Asclepius stands on the upper terrace where there had been a sacred grove of Apollo (yearly reports: *AA* 16, 1901, 131ff; *AA* 18, 1903, 1ff; 180ff; *AA* 20, 1905, 1ff) (R. Herzog and P. Schazmann, *Kos, Ergebnisse der deutschen Ausgrabungen und Forschungen, Bd. I: Asklepieion,* Berlin 1932. There seem to have been no further volumes). The Italians worked on the site during their occupation. Excavations included a first century Roman bath. In 1967 Hope Simpson noted evidence for what is probably a small Bronze Age settlement on a plateau above and southwest of the Asclepieion (*Dod.* 2, 58).

In 1967, Hope Simpson noted Late Neolithic or Early Bronze Age sherds and obsidian of the Yali type on the badly eroded Troulli spur about 3 km east of Kos.

At Asklupi south of Kos, Morricone excavated three late EB age pithoi burials (*Boll. d'Arte* 35, 1950, 324ff) and Hope Simpson noted evidence of a prehistoric settlement on the nearby acropolis (*Dod.* 2, 57). At Mesaria along the road west of Kos, Nikolaides reported a similar pithos burial (*AR* 1958, 16) (*Dod.* 2, 58).

At Asfendiou on the slopes of Mt. Dikaios the Italians excavated a Byzantine basilica and a temple of Demeter and Kore. Northwest of the village of Zia, south of Asfendiou, Hope Simpson noted a Bronze Age site (*Dod.* 2, 58).

At the medieval fortress on the Palaiopyli Kastro at Amaniou, Hope Simpson noted Mycenaean sherds and a section of Cyclopean wall (*Dod.* 2, 59-60). Konstantinopoulos and Nikolaides excavated a ruined Mycenaean tomb at Ayia Paraskevi near Pyli. Vases are of the range LH IIIA2–IIIC1 (*Dod.* 2, 60).

At the Stavros chapel near Pyli are the remains of a heroon of Charmylos, of Hellenistic date, excavated by the Italians (*Memorie dell' Istituto storico-arch. di Rodi*, 1, 1933, 103ff).

The site of Astypalaia, which was succeeded after 366 by the Hellenistic deme of Isthmus, was located in 1898 by Duncan Mackenzie at the Panaghia Palatiane chapel near Kephalos (*BSA* 4, 1897–8, 95ff). Herzog cleared the ancient foundations on which the chapel rests in 1902 (*AA* 1903, 2ff) and in 1928 Laurenzi excavated a Hellenistic temple and theatre (*Historia* 5, 1931, 625ff).There are remains of a part of a circuit wall and bastion, and sherds of all periods from perhaps the 9th century through Roman times were noted (*BSA* 52, 1957, 123ff).

The Aspropetro cave south of Kephalos was excavated by the Italians in 1922. There is evidence of continuous use from Neolithic through Roman times. Stone implements and obsidian were found, some Mycenaean sherds, and plentiful Geometric sherds. By the 4th century BC the cave was dedicated to Pan and the Nymphs (*Clara Rhodos* 1, 1928, 99ff) (*Ann.* 8-9, 1925–6, 159ff).

A.N. Modona "L'Isola di Coo nell' Antichità classica," (*Memorie dell' Istituto storico-arch. di Rodi* I, 1933) is a history and survey of Kos. A summary of Italian excavations has been made (*Historia* 5, 1931, 479ff).

LEROS: Leros has been described by Ludwig Bürchner (*Die Insel Leros*, München, 1898), Dawkins and Wace (*BSA* 12, 1905-6, 172ff), Bean and Cook (*BSA* 52, 1957, 134ff) and J.L. Benson (*Ancient Leros;* Greek, Roman and Byzantine Monographs no. 3, Durham, N.C. 1963), also by Gerola (*Ann.* 2, 1916, 61ff) and Susini (*Ann.* 41-2, 1963–4, 300ff). Despite its geographical closeness to Kalymnos, Leros was Ionian and Milesian, while the islands to the south were Dorian.

The Kastro, called Phrourion, on which there are the remains of a castle of the Knights of St. John, was the acropolis for the Classical and later settlement at Ayia Marina below it. In 1967, Hope Simpson noted

Mycenaean sherds on the northwest slopes (*Dod.* 2, 54).

In the area of Partheni in the north there was a temple of the Parthenos, destroyed in the beginning of the 11th century. It was reported by early travellers; Bernard Randolph (*The Present State of the Islands,* Oxford, 1687) reported seeing at least 20 whole pillars. Since then, the remains have entirely disappeared and the site of the temple is unknown, though there are several possible sites in the area (Benson, op.cit., 16ff). On the central of three small promontories extending into Partheni Bay, Hope Simpson in 1967 found prehistoric sherds, probably EB age, and similar sherds outside a cave about one kilometer inland (*Dod.* 2, 52-3).

On the Xerokampos hill in the south there once were extensive remains of fortification walls (*BSA* 12, 1905–6, 173ff) but these have since largely disappeared. There are still a few remains of Hellenistic date, and a stretch of what appears to be a Cyclopean wall, but Hope Simpson's intensive search produced no Mycenaean sherds and this wall also may be later (Benson, op.cit., 27ff) (*Dod.* 2, 54).

LIPSOI: The island has been described by Bean and Cook (*BSA* 52, 1957, 135ff) and R. Hope Simpson (*Dod.* 2, 512).

At Ayios Nikolaos, the modern village at the east end of Sokoro Bay, there are 5th–4th century sherds, and perhaps 7th–6th century ones. This covers a small area, and is perhaps the site of the sanctuary of Apollo Lepsieus rather than a town. There are Doric and Ionic column drums nearby at the Ayia Markella chapel.

At the Kastro inland above the village there are remains of ancient fortification walls, foundations within them, and terraces on the south slopes. An altar to Zeus Genethlios was found at the site, and Archaic, 5th–4th century black-glazed, and Hellenistic sherds. The settlement appears to have been quite large. Hope Simpson noted sherds which might be Middle or Late Bronze Age.

NISYROS: Nisyros has been discussed by Ross (*Reisen* 2, 72ff), Dawkins and Wace (*BSA* 12, 1905–6, 165ff), Fraser and Bean (*The Rhodian Peraea and Islands,* 147ff), Bean and Cook, (*BSA* 52, 1957, 118ff) and Hope Simpson (*Dod.* 1, 169).

The ancient town was on the Kastro above Mandraki in the northwest. Along with medieval remains, considerable stretches of the ancient fortress wall with towers and a gate can be traced, and remains of ancient terrace walls within. Sherds go back perhaps to the late 7th century. Hope Simpson and Lazenby found sherds which might be either Mycenaean or

Archaic, also obsidian chips of the Yali type. A Cycladic idol is reported to have come from Nisyros (*BSA* 52, 1957, 119 note 217).

In 1932 across the valley on the east of the Kastro the Italians excavated burials in a Classical and Hellenistic cemetery, Roman tombs with sculptured altars, and a series of cremations dating from the end of the 7th century (*Clara Rhodos* 6, 1931, 471ff).

Remains of late Roman baths at the hot springs at Panaghia Thermiani near Pali were described by Pantelides (*BCH* 1891, 488).

PATMOS: An early description of ancient remains was given by B. Pace (*Ann.* 1, 1914, 371ff). Kastelli, in the center of the island west of the main harbor of Skala, was the only important ancient settlement. The site was cleared by Kondis of the Greek Archeological Service from 1957–59 (*PAE* 1958, 241; 1959, 196), and Hope Simpson visited the island in 1967, finding Bronze Age and Geometric sherds. The ancient fortifications are probably of the 3rd century (*Dod.* 2, 48ff).

RHODES: General bibliography on Rhodes includes:
1. E. Biliotti et L'Abbé Cottret, *L'Ile de Rhodes*, Rhodes 1881.
2. R.U. Inglieri, *Carta Archeologica dell' Isola di Rodi*, Fiorenze, 1936: A gazetteer with bibliography of known sites, excavated and unexcavated. Many of the sites listed by Inglieri have not been published elsewhere, and are not included in the following listing. His topographical notes are not always accurate, and many of the sites he mentioned cannot now be located.
3. R. Hope Simpson and J.F. Lazenby, "Notes from the Dodecanese III," *BSA* 68, 1973, 127ff, on a survey of Rhodes conducted in 1968 and 1970. Whenever possible, Hope Simpson and Lazenby corrected and clarified Inglieri's notes.

Much of the archaeological exploration of Rhodes, as with the rest of the Dodecanese, has been carried out by the Italians. Reports on their excavations have been published in the ten volumes of the series *Clara Rhodos*, published from 1928 to 1941 (abbreviated as *CR*), and in volumes two and three of the *Memorie dell' Istituto storico-arch. di Rodi*, 1938 (abbreviated as *Memorie 2* and *3*).

Notices of excavations have been published in the relevant years of *Annuario* and *Bolletino d'Arte*.

The following list of sites proceeds generally in an anti-clockwise direction around the island.

In 1916 Maiuri identified the acropolis of the city of Rhodes on the hill known as Mt. Smith or Mt. Ayios Stefanos and excavated a stadium (*CR* 1, 1928, 49). In 1917–29 Jacopi excavated on the acropolis, working particularly on the theatre (*Memorie* 2, 1938, 25ff). In 1937 Laurenzi excavated the temple of Delian Apollo. The Italians studied the ancient fortifications of the city in the early 1920's. In 1922 they found a temple of Aphrodite in the Arsenal Square in the Old City, in 1922 a temple of Athena Polias and Zeus Polieus, and in 1925 a sanctuary of Dionysos (*CR* 1, 1928, 45ff).

Since 1951 the Greeks, particularly the Ephor Kondis, have been working yearly in Rhodes city. Attention has been particularly given to the fortifications and to the Hippodamian plan of the city. Others working in the area have been K. Phatourou, G. Konstantinopoulos, I. Zervoudakis, and C. Grossmann (*PAE* 1951, 224ff; 1952, 547ff; 1953, 275ff) (*AD* 16, 1960, *Chr.* 275ff; *AD* 17, 1961–2, *Chr.* 301ff, and annually since). Kondis has published a study of the city walls (*AD* 18, 1963, *Mel.* 77ff) and Konstantinopoulos has reported on the fortifications' towers (*AE* 1967, 115ff). Mrs. C. Grossmann has published a plan of the Hippodamian city which embodied the results of the previous twelve years' work (*AD* 24, 1969, *Chr.* 451ff). In 1968 Konstantinopoulos and Zervoudakis worked in the necropoleis of Rhodes. In the Phaneromeni area they found 91 Hellenistic and Roman pit graves, and outside the walls on the road to Lindos, graves dating from the period after the foundation of the city. Konstantinopoulos reported on his discoveries in 1969 and 1973 (*AD* 25, *Chr.* 2, 500ff) (*Ergon* 1973, 101ff).

In the area of Ialysos there are numerous ancient sites. The northwest coastal plain has the largest concentration of Mycenaean remains on the island (cf. *Dod.* 3, 143, 155ff). The remains on the acropolis of Ialysos are mainly Classical and later, though 9th–5th century votives have been found, and Neolithic sherds were discovered at the extreme northwest end of the site in 1925. Other remains on the acropolis included the 3rd century BC temple of Athena Ialysia and a 4th century BC monumental fountain. The area was visited by Biliotti in 1868–71 (Biliotti and Cottret, op.cit., 386ff) but was only identified in 1913. The Italians excavated in 1913–14 (the temple) and in 1923–26, with some reconstruction being done (Maiuri, *CR* 1, 1928, 72ff) (*Boll. d'Arte* 3, 1923–4, 237ff; *Boll. d'Arte* 6, 1926–7, 331-2: Neolithic sherds). At Trianda a habitation site of Minoan character, if not a Minoan colony, was partially excavated in 1935–36 (G. Monaco, *Memorie* 3, 1938, 57ff) (*CR* 10, 1941, 41ff) (cf. A. Furumark, *Op. Arch.* 6, 1950, 150ff). There are three strata, beginning with MM. The site flourished from LM I A to LM III A1, in the last period gradually assuming a more Mycenaean character. There is a little evidence for LH III A2–III B1 continuation or reoccupation, but the chief Mycenaean center may have been closer to the Mycenaean cemeteries (*Dod.* 3, 135-6).

Spectacular results have come from the necropoleis in the area of Ialysos, which range from the Mycenaean period through Roman times.

The Mycenaean cemeteries are located at Moschou Vounara and Makria Vounara between Trianda and the acropolis of Ialysos. Alfred Billioti and Auguste Salzmann excavated 41 graves in 1868–71 (E. Biliotti and Cottrett, op.cit., 386ff) (*B.M. Cat. of Greek and Etruscan Vases,* I.1, 1925, nos. 801-970). The cemeteries were frequently looted until the Italians began systematic excavations, carried out by Maiuri in 1914 and 1922.

Jacopi directed the work from 1924–28 (*Ann.* 2, 1916, 271ff) (*CR* 1, 1928, 56ff) (major reports: *Ann.* 6-7, 1923–4, 86ff; *Ann.* 13-14, 1930–31, 254ff). The graves are generally chamber tombs of LH IIIB–IIIC date. Moschou Vounara may have been the center of a habitation site: there are traces of rough walls and sherds were picked up (*Dod.* 3, 137). Various groups of graves have been excavated northwest of the acropolis of Ialysos (Inglieri nos. 18-23) at various times from 1913 to 1936: a cemetery of Geometric and Archaic cremations was discovered at Daphni in 1913 (*Boll. d'Arte* 8, 1914, 224ff), and was further excavated in 1922, 1925 and 1934–5 (*CR* 8, 1936, 29ff). Another similar group of graves was excavated at Zambico in 1922–26 (*Ann.* 6-7, 1923–24, 288ff) (*CR* 1, 1928, 65ff). A report on 341 Geometric and Archaic graves excavated from 1924 to 1928 has been published by Jacopi (*CR* 3, 1929, 1ff). A large necropolis of Archaic cremations, changing to inhumations in the second half of the 6th century was excavated in 1916, and in 1934–5 at Marmaro (*Ann.* 6-7, 1923–4, 257ff) (major report in *CR* 8, 1936, 64ff). Of later burials, a group of 6th–5th century burials (*CR* 3, 1929, 204ff), fifth century Hellenistic and Roman graves (*Boll. d'Arte ser.* 2, 8, 1928, 328ff) were excavated in the years 1924–27.

Two km northwest of Maritsa near the Rhodes airport, Hope Simpson noted Mycenaean sherds and a chamber tomb, which is probably the site 'Coccala' where three chamber tombs with dromoi were excavated in 1926 (*Boll. d'Arte, ser.* 2, 6, 1926–7, 331) (*Memorie* 2, 1938, 51) (*Dod.* 3, 139).

Slightly to the east of Paradhisi, previously known as Villanova, there was a late Roman and medieval site at Palaiochora. Traces of habitation, a Roman necropolis, and a rich deposit of early 2nd century BC Rhodian amphora were found in the area (*Ann.*4-5, 1921–2, 249ff). In 1913 Pace excavated Mycenaean chamber tombs in the area (*Ann.* 1, 1914, 369-70) (*Boll. d'Arte* 10, 1916, 87ff). The vases were of transitional LH IIIA1-2. The area was visited by Hope Simpson and Lazenby in 1968 and they attempted to relocate the sites of these excavations (*Dod.* 3, 138). Laurenzi noted a Mycenaean tholos tomb somewhere near Villanova (*Memorie* 2, 1938, 49, 51) but Hope Simpson could not relocate it.

Off the road to Soroni, in the area of Tolon, are the remains of a theatre and a late 5th-early 4th century temple of Apollo Eretimios. It was noted by Ross (*Reisen* 3, 1845, 100ff) and excavated by the Italians (*CR* 2, 1932, 77ff). At the Ayios Ioannis Theologos Chapel about 1 km southwest of Tolon are fragments of columns, triglyphs, some Archaic tombs, and a

Mycenaean chamber tomb which produced LH IIIA1 vases (*CR* 6, 1931, 44, 49) (*Dod.* 3, 140).

South of Soroni late Mycenaean cist graves are reported (*Memorie* 2, 1938, 51) and Hope Simpson noted Classical tombs in the area (*Dod.* 3, 140-1).

In the area of the Anifora hill near Kalavarda, east of Kamerios, A. Furtwängler excavated 2 Mycenaean chamber tombs in 1886 (*Jahrbuch* 1, 1886, 133), Another was excavated in 1913 (*Ann.* 1, 1914, 369)(*Boll. d'Arte* 9, 1915, 297ff) and five more in 1930 (*CR* 6, 1931, 133ff). The pottery ranges from LH IIIA2–IIIC1. Hope Simpson noted sherds, perhaps from a settlement, possibly MM, and of Mycenaean, Geometric, and later periods (*Dod.* 3, 141ff).

A. Salzmann and A. Biliotti excavated on the acropolis of Kameiros and in the nearby cemeteries in 1858–65, and Biliotti alone in 1880 (E. Biliotti et L' Abbé Cottrett, op.cit., esp. 395ff). The necropolis was at Papa-tis-lures east of Kameiros, and Mycenaean, Archaic, and Classical graves were found (A. Salzmann, *Nécropole de Camiros, Journal des fouilles 1858–1865,* Paris, 1875) (cf. Loeschke, *AM* 6, 1881, 1ff) (cf. Launay, *RA* 27, 1895, 82ff). Italians worked both on the acropolis and at various cemeteries in 1912–3 (*Ann.* 1, 1914, 386) (*Boll. d'Arte* 8, 1914, 226ff; *Boll. d'Arte* 9, 1915, 283ff), and from 1928–1930 (*CR* 4, 1931, 1ff; *CR* 6, 1931, 9ff). On the acropolis are remains of the temple of Athena Kameiras, a 3rd century BC temenos with remains of a Doric temple, a large Hellenistic agora or stoa, a large cistern, and Hellenistic houses on the slopes. There are also proto-Geometric tombs on the acropolis.

In the northern foothills of Mt. Profitis Ilias, Mycenaean tombs and various Classical and later remains in the area of Salakos are noted in Inglieri (nos. 117-127), apparently unexcavated or unpublished. South of Mt. Profitis Ilias, about 4 km west of Apollona, 7 Mycenaean chamber tombs with LH IIIA2–IIIB vases were excavated by the Italians in 1915 (Maiuri, *Ann.* 2, 1916, 298ff; *Ann.* 6-7, 1923–4, 248ff). About 1 km northeast of these tombs a fortified Classical settlement was found (*Ann.* 2, 1916, 300-2) and LH IIIB vases were reported probably from this vicinity (Jacopi, *ILN,* 20 May, 1933). Hope Simpson and Lazenby visited the area and their notes help clarify the location of the various sites (*Dod.* 3, 143-4).

Along the coast southwest of Kameiros, a Mycenaean chamber tomb with dromos was excavated on the Melissaki hill (*Ann.* 6-7, 1923–4, 252-3), and Hope Simpson noted evidence of Hellenistic and late Roman habitation in 1970 (*Dod.* 3, 144-5).

At Kritinia, formerly Castello, a necropolis of chamber tombs was partially excavated by Biliotti (Biliotti and Cottrett, op.cit., 420) and by the Italians (*Boll. d'Arte* 8, 1914, 231ff). At Petronia nearby, Biliotti also worked in an Archaic and Classical necropolis (op.cit., 420). North of Kritinia, on the rocky knoll of Kastraki, is a good stretch of fortification wall, probably Hellenistic, noted by Biliotti (Biliotti and Cottrett, op.cit., 413ff) and Pernier (*Boll. d'Arte*, 8, 1914, 230ff). Hope Simpson and Lazenby noted Mycenaean sherds nearby, and Kastraki was probably the Mycenaean settlement site to which the Mycenaean tombs in the vicinity belonged (*Dod.* 3, 145). Numerous tombs of all periods from Mycenaean to Hellenistic and later are listed by Inglieri in the Kritinia area (nos. 138-141, 146-153) but most are not now visible.

On the promontory at the west end of the bay of Lagonia, west of Kastraki, is a carved façade in Lycian style overlooking the coast, and the surface of the promontory is covered with foundations and cuttings, probably for tombs (Biliotti and Cottrett, op.cit., 14ff) (*Boll. d'Arte* 8, 1914, 235ff) (*Dod.* 3, 145-6).

On the summit of Mt. Atavyros, the highest peak in Rhodes, are the remains of the sanctuary of Zeus Atavyros. There are traces of a peribolos and a Hellenistic propylon. It was noted by Ross (*Reisen* 3, 1845, 107), Biliotti (Biliotti and Cottrett, op.cit., 429ff) and excavated by the Italians in 1927 (Jacopi, *CR* 1, 1928, 88ff).

Ayios Fokas, northwest of Siana, is the center of a group of ancient remains, particularly Classical and Hellenistic, and was perhaps the ancient deme of the Kymisaleis. At Ayios Fokas there are remains of ancient circuit walls, and a small temple, probably Hellenistic. In the Vasiliki plain slightly to the west there are remains of ancient buildings and an enclosure wall. On the Marmaroulia hill to the south of Ayios Fokas, traces of wall, and Archaic and 5th–4th century pottery have been found. The Ayios Fokas vicinity was visited by Biliotti (Biliotti and Cottrett, op.cit., 439ff) and was excavated by Italians in 1914–15 (*Ann.* 1, 1914, 365ff; *Ann.* 2, 1916, 285ff) (*CR* 1, 1928, 83ff). Hope Simpson and Lazenby noted sherds of either Late Neolithic or Early Bronze Age (*Dod.* 3, 146). In the Kymisala plain below Ayios Fokas on the south are extensive cemeteries, largely of Archaic to Roman date, though Mycenaean vases are also reported (Biliotti and Cottrett, op.cit., 439, 442) (*CR* 1, 1928, 83ff) (*Dod.* 3, 146-7). Miss Zervoudakis excavated a 5th–4th century tomb there (*AD* 24, 1969, *Chr.* 480ff). The nearby beach at Glyphada has traces of habitation and 4th–3rd century tombs (*Ann.* 2, 1916, 296) (*Dod.* 3, 147).

K.F. Kinch, supported by the Danish Carlsberg Fund, excavated an Archaic town at Vroulia, on the southern tip of the island, in 1907–8. The town had a short existence, from about 700 to 560 BC, and could hardly have been inhabited by more than forty people at a time (K.F. Kinch, *Fouilles de Vroulia*, Berlin 1914). North of Vroulia, Kinch also excavated Mycenaean tombs northwest of the village of Kattavia, between the village and the Ayios Minas chapel (Kinch, op.cit. 2ff) and there is evidence for a Mycenaean settlement on the Ayios Minas spur (*Dod.* 3. 147-8). At Karavi, about 2.5 km southeast of Kattavia, Kinch excavated a Mycenaean cemetery (Kinch, op. cit., 3).

Near the Zoodhochos Piyi chapel at Plimmiri Bay on the coast southeast of Lachania are ancient remains, perhaps ancient Ixia. Biliotti visited the area and excavated ancient tombs (Biliotti, op. cit., 424ff). There are remains of a circuit wall, and mainly Hellenistic sherds are reported, though some may be prehistoric (*Dod.* 3, 149).

At Ayia Sotira at Yenadhi, Mycenaean chamber tombs with dromoi have been reported (Maiuri, *Ann.* 6-7, 1923–4, 253) and there is evidence of a Hellenistic and Roman settlement (*Dod.* 3, 149). Inland from Yenadhi, on the south side of the road to Vati, above the Evrymachia spring, abundant Hellenistic and Roman sherds were found over an extensive area (ibid. 150) and further inland, about 1.5 km east of Vati, a Mycenaean cemetery was partially excavated by Kinch (Kinch, op. cit., 2ff) and later by the Italians (Maiuri, op.cit., 253ff). Pottery ranges from LH IIIA2-IIIC1.

North of the village of Lardos, west of Lindos, a large Mycenaean cemetery, mostly looted, produced LH IIIA2–IIIC1 vases (*Ann.* 6-7, 1923–4, fig. 159–60) (*Dod.* 3, 150-1).

About 1 km southwest of Pilona at Ambelia, a Mycenaean chamber tomb was excavated in 1929–30 (Jacopi, *Ann.* 13-14, 1930–31, 335ff) (*Historia* 5, 1931, 468).

The Acropolis of Lindos was visited by Ross, who copied inscriptions but did not excavate (*AZ* 9, 1851, 281ff). In 1902 a Danish expedition led by K.F. Kinch began excavations on the acropolis and neighboring areas. There were three major campaigns until 1905, and then some supplementary work until 1914. (Preliminary reports: *Bull. de l'Acad. R. de Danemark*, 1-6, 1902, 1912) (Final reports: Chr. Blinkenberg, K.F. Kinch, E. Dyggve, *Lindos, Fouilles et Recherches 1902–1914*, Fondation Carlsberg, Copenhagen, vol. 1: *Acropolis, Petits Objets*, Berlin 1931. E. Dyggve visited Lindos in 1952 in preparation of vol. 3: *Le Sanctuaire d'Athana Lindia et l'Architecture Lindienne*, Berlin 1960). Most of the buildings on the acropolis, including the temple of Athena, a propylon, walls, and a theatre, postdate a fire of about 350–333 BC. The temple replaced a sixth century temple. The site had been occupied since prehistoric times. Late Neolothic or Early Bronze Age and Mycenaean pottery was found (*Lindos* I, 60ff) (*Dod.* 3, 151-2). The Italians studied and restored the temple (*Memorie* 2, 1938, 9ff)(*Boll. d'Arte*, ser. 2,6, 1926–7, 328ff). At Ayios Aemilianos on the northwest side of the harbor is a round structure, 28.25 m in circumference, known as the Tomb of Cleobulos, which is similar to some mainland Carian tombs (Kinch, op. cit., 1, 1902, 86ff) (*Ann.* 4-5, 1921–2, 457ff).

Archaic chamber tombs were excavated at 'Plakato', 2 km southeast of Malona (Maiuri, op. cit. 253).

On the Anagros hill north of Archangelos village Late Neolithic or Early Bronze Age sherds were noted (*Dod.* 3, 152-3). Southwest of the town two Mycenaean chamber tombs with LH IIIA2–IIIC1 vases were excavated near the Petrokopio quarry (*BCH* 73, 1949, 535) (cf. Kharitonides, *AD* 18, 1963, *Mel.* 135ff).

On Eremokastro at Kallithies Zancani excavated briefly (*Ann.* 6-7, 1923–4, 564). There are walls of Cyclopean type, but of uncertain date, though apparently prehistoric sherds were noted. There are reports of Mycenaean finds (Inglieri nos. 58, 59) (*Memorie* 2, 1938, 51) but these are unconfirmed (cf. *Dod.* 3, 154-5). LH IIIA2–B1 vases are reported from Koskinou (*AD* 18, 1963, *Mel.* 133-4).

SARIA: Saria, the Ancient Saros, north of Karpathos, was possibly as sparsely occupied in antiquity as it is now (*Dod.* 1, 168, note 126). The ancient site at Palatia on the east coast is described by Dawkins (*BSA* 9, 1902-3, 206ff). Most remains are medieval, though the possibly 5th century AD predecessor of the present chapel of Ayia Sophia was constructed with a great number of ancient marble fragments.

Bent examined rock-cut tombs in the south of the island and found bits of pottery similar to the presumably Classical ware he found on Karpathos (*JHS* 6, 1885, 239).

A Bronze Age dagger, chisel and a flat celt from Saria were presented to the British Museum by W.R. Paton in 1889.

SYME: Syme is discussed by Bean and Cook (*BSA* 52, 1957, 116), Fraser and Bean (*The Rhodian Peraea,* 139ff) and Hope Simpson and Lazenby (*Dod.* 1, 168-9; *Dod.* 2, 63).

On the Kastro above the harbor in the northeast are traces of two circuit walls. Fifth and fourth century sherds, and possibly Archaic ones were found. The site has the appearance of a Mycenaean citadel, and several possibly Mycenaean sherds were noted, and at least one definitely LH IIIA or B (*Dod.* 2, 63).

TELOS: The chief ancient site on Telos is the Kastro at Megalochorio in the north, which was the ancient acropolis. The site was visited by Bent in 1884–5 (*JHS* 6, 1885, 233ff) who described the site and excavated two probably Classical cemeteries. Dawkins placed their probable location on the slopes between Megalochorio village and the landing place (*BSA* 12, 1905-6, 163). The Kastro was described by Gerola (*Ann.* 2, 1916, 13ff) and thoroughly investigated by Dawkins and Wace (*BSA* 12, 1905-6, 159ff), Bean and Cook (*BSA* 52, 1957, 116-8), Susini (*Ann.* 41-2, 1963-4, 261ff) and visited by Hope Simpson in 1967 (*Dod*. 2, 63ff). Fifth century and later sherds were found. There are considerable remains of city walls, terraces, and the city on the south slope, but these remains are probably 4th century at the earliest. There is a medieval castle on the site.

On the Kastello at Livadhia there are some stretches of ancient fortifications, probably Hellenistic, and Classical and Hellenistic sherds. In 1957 Hope Simpson found some very worn prehistoric sherds, probably of EB Age, and two obsidian chips at the north end of the site (*Dod*. 2, 68).

The Cyclades

AMORGOS: Little systematic exploration of cemeteries or settlements of historical periods has taken place.

In the latter part of the 19th century, Dümmler and Tsountas excavated and reported on prehistoric finds on the island, mostly Early Cycladic graves. Sites included are: Ayia Paraskevi in the southwest; ancient Arkesine; Dokathismata, southeast of Arkesine; Phoinikies, Kato Akrotiri; Xilokeratidi, Kapros, and Vouni in the central part; Aigiale in the north; Notina, Stavros, Kokkina Chomata, Kapsala, and Ayios Georgios along the southeast coastline (Dümmler, *AM* 11, 1886, 15ff) (C. Tsountas, "Kykladika I," *AE* 1898, 152ff, 208ff).

Dümmler worked particularly on the site of ancient Arkesine (Kastri), located north of Vroutsi in the southern part of the island. Graves in the area produced pottery of a period transitional between EC and MC. The French under M. Deschamps excavated Greek and Roman remains at Arkesine in 1888 (Deschamps, *BCH* 12, 1888, 326ff) (*Athenaeum,* May 12, 1888), and there is a Hellenistic tower, but the sherds also indicate occupation since prehistoric times (E.M. Bossert, *Festschrift P. Goessler,* Berlin, 1954, 23) (K. Scholes, *BSA* 51, 1956, 11, 31, 34).

The French also excavated Classical remains at Minoa, in the Katapola Bay area in 1888 (Deschamps, op.cit., 324ff). In 1949 Kondoleon and L. Politis found fifth and fourth century remains, and in 1961 N. Zafeiropoulos found late Archaic material (*AR* 1961, 22). Early Cycladic occupation of this region is attested by several of the cemeteries excavated by Dümmler and Tsountas. Bosanquet purchased an LH III stirrup-jar at Xilokeratidi (*Corpus Vasorum Antiquorum,* Gt. Britain, plate 484, 11) on the northern side of Katapola Bay, and there was probably a Mycenaean site in the Katapola Bay area, as it has the best anchorage in the island (Scholes, op. cit., 11). Zafeiropoulos found a plundered Mycenaean chamber tomb near Katapola in 1961.

Another site is that of ancient Aigiale (Vigli) near Tholaria in the north-

39

west, 1 km from the sea (*AM* 11, 1886, 40), visited by Deschamps in 1888 (op.cit., 327). Kondoleon and Politis worked there in 1949. There are walls of Archaic or Classical date, but the sherds testify to occupation from prehistoric times to Late Classical (Scholes, op.cit., 11).

Mrs. F. Zafeiropoulos also surveyed the area (*AD* 22, 1967, *Chr.* 2, 465ff) (*AAA* 3, 1970, 48ff) (*AAA* 6, 1973, 351ff). R.Z.N. Barber of the British School explored the island in 1974.

ANDROS: The ancient city of Andros was located on the west coast at Palaiopolis, and there are a few Classical remains today including a wall, waterway, and submerged piers. A statue of Hermes was uncovered here in 1832. Nothing prehistoric has been found, although this may be due to covering by alluvial deposits, as the Classical remains themselves were found at great depths (J.T. Bent, *Aegean Islands,* 1885, 289). There is a report of LH IIIA–B sherds in the museum of Andros town (K. Scholes, *BSA* 51, 1956, 11, 31), reportedly from Palaiopolis, but Miss Scholes feels that a more suitable prehistoric settlement would be located at Gaviron, Andros, or Korthi, with more sheltered bays (ibid.).

In 1960, excavations were begun on a Geometric settlement at Zagora on the west coast in the southern part of the island by N. Kondoleon and N. Zafeiropoulos; late Geometric pottery and pithoi were recovered (*Eleutheria,* November 20, 1960). In 1961 they continued excavations of three houses and uncovered a temple.

In 1967 and 1969, the excavations were continued at Zagora, under A. Cambitoglou, and sponsored by the University of Sydney. The finds indicated occupation in the 8th, and abandonment in the 7th century. The temple was shown to be built in the 6th century, probably after the settlement was abandoned (*AR* 1967–68, 17) (*BCH* 92, 1968, 951ff) (*Ergon* 1969, 131ff) (A. Cambitoglou et al; *Zagora* 1, Sidney University Press, 1971). In 1973, Cambitoglou returned to the island for a four month study season.

ANTIPAROS: J.T. Bent excavated about forty Cycladic graves on the island in 1884 and described the contents (J.T. Bent, *Aegean Islands,* 1885) (*JHS* 5, 1884, 42ff).

Tsountas excavated 50 EC cist graves at Krassades ("Kykladika I," *AE* 1898, 161-2).

There are two known Late Neolithic sites on the island: Vouni, a settlement of the Saliagos culture (Evans and Renfrew, *Excavations at Saliagos, BSA* Suppl. vol. no. 5, 1968, 71ff), and a cave in which G. Bakalakis found Neolithic sherds (*AA* 1969, 126ff).

DELOS: The excavations on Delos by the French School at Athens are one of the oldest continuous series of archaeological explorations undertaken in Greece. All periods are represented, back into the 3rd millenium BC (see particularly A. Plassart, *Exploration archéologique de Délos*, 11). A settlement of the Early and Middle Cycladic periods has been located on the Kynthos hill site. In Late Cycladic times, the settlement moved northwest to flatter land in the Temenos area. Many Mycenaean finds were made under the Artemision. The French have uncovered numerous other buildings through Roman times.

The first excavations by the French School were begun by C.A. Lebègue in 1872, followed up by Stamatakis in 1873. Since the remains on the lower part of the island were covered, the original work was devoted to higher ground on Mount Kynthos. In 1877, Théophile Homolle began the excavations in the plain which continue to this day. Another important archaeologist was Maurice Holleaux; credit should also be given to the Duke of Loubat, who financially sponsored some of the excavations. *Bulletin de Correspondance Hellènique*, Suppl. I, 1973, *Études Déliennes*, published on the hundredth anniversary of the beginning of the French Delos excavations, includes a summary of their history.

Other archaeologists working on the island through the years include J. Chamonard, Gallet de Santerre, P. Roussel. V. de Schoeffer, S. Molinier, J. Hartzfeld, M. Lacroix, C. Dugas, R. Vallois, G. Leroux, M. Bulard, F. Courby, G. Fougères, C. Picard, F. Durrbach, A. Jardé, C. Avezou, W. Dèonna, J. Replat, Devambez, F. Robert, Coufry, Roger, J. Tréheux, C. Dugas, J. Marcadé, N.M. Kondoleon, A. Orlandos, P. Corbin, C. LeRoy, P. Bruneau, J. Ducat, C. Vatin, A. Bovon, G. Donnay, U.T. Bezerra, G. Siebert, S. Reinach, R. Demangel, G. Daux, and M.-Th. Couilloud.

Publications regarding excavations on Delos have been numerous. A very good summary of publications is listed in *Cambridge Ancient History* (*CAH* 8, 792ff). Important publications are listed in the *Oxford Classical Dictionary*. Annual reports are recorded in the *BCH*; and since 1909 in a series of excavation reports entitled *Exploration Archéologique de Délos* (published by E. de Boccard, since no. 6).

DESPOTIKO: In 1897 Tsountas excavated an Early Cycladic cemetery at Leivadhi, an EC settlement at Kheiromylos, and an EC cemetery and settlement at 'Zoumbana' or 'Zoumbaria' (*AE* 1898, 162ff). In 1960 N. Zafeiropoulos excavated twenty EC tombs at Zoumbana, all slab-lined cist graves, with one exception, having stone built walls. Vases of the early 'Pelos' type were found. At 'Mandra', fragments of a kouros and of an Archaic temple were found (*BCH* 1960, 814).

DONOUSA: Mrs. F. Zafeiropoulos reported on traces of two prehistoric settlements at Achita ton Agrilion and Kato Mylos Platyvolias (*AD* 22, 1967, *Chr.* 2, 467).

In 1968–72 she excavated a fortified settlement of the Geometric period on the promontory, and a cemetery whose graves produced Geometric vases (*AD* 24, 1969, *Chr.* 2, 390ff) (*AD* 25, 1970, *Chr.* 2, 426ff) (*AAA* 4, 1971, 210ff) (*AAA* 6, 1973, 256ff). The Geometric pottery appeared to have closer affiliation with Rhodes and Eastern Greece than with the other Cyclades.

HERAKLEA: Mrs. F. Zafeiropoulos reported traces of a prehistoric settlement at Kambos Ayiou Athanasiou in the north of the island, traces of a large prehistoric settlement at Ayios Mamas, EC cist graves in the southwest, and prehistoric sherds on the Kastro (*AD* 22, 1967, *Chr.* 2, 465-6).

IOS: Graindor of the French School reported EC cist graves containing folded arm figurines (*BCH* 28, 1904, 309).

KEA: In 1811–12 P.O. Bröndsted explored Kea, and excavated at the site of ancient Karthaia on the southeast coast. (Bröndsted, *Reisen und Untersuchungen in Griechenland*, Paris, 1826; vol. 1 deals with Kea/Keos). In 1903 and 1904 the French School, supported by the Belgian Government, excavated at Karthaia, including a prehistoric grave, and the temples of Athena and Apollo (P. Graindor, *BCH* 29, 1905, 329ff) (*BCH* 30, 1906, 92ff) (*Museé Belge* 25, 1921, 83ff). In 1962 Doumas re-examined the fifth century temple of Athena, uncovering some Hellenistic votive statuettes, and the temple of Apollo (*Kathimerini* Feb. 2, 1963) (*BCH* 89, 1965, 858ff).

The ancient city of Koressia with a temple of Apollo Sminthios is near modern Livadi or Koressia. In 1929 Stavropoulos excavated an Archaic cemetery at Livadi and found a large kouros figure (*AR* 1929–30, 244). Welter (*AA* 1954, 51ff) excavated at Koressia including the Archaic temple, and he mentions vaguely 'prehistoric' remains found below the temple. Graindor had noted the remains of a Cyclopean wall at Koressia (*Museé Belge,* 15, 1911, 62).

Welter also examined the remains of ancient Ioulis, the Kastro of the modern Khora or Kea town, including the city walls, the remains of a temple of Apollo, a large Archaic statue of a lion, and a lion relief (*AA* 1954, 70ff). He also located 27 ancient towers, probably Hellenistic, the most notable of which is at the ruined monastery of Ayia Marina (ibid. 87ff) (cf. Graindor, *Museé Belge* 25, 1921, 113ff).

On Cape Kephala on the north coast Tsountas excavated numerous prehistoric graves, ("Kykladika 1," *AE* 1898, 137ff). The finds were discussed by T.W. Jacobson (*AJA* 68, 1964, 196), and J.E. Coleman concluded tentatively that they belonged to a late stage of the Late Neolithic period (*AJA* 78, 1974, 335ff). In conjunction with the American School excavation at Ayia Irini, J.L. Caskey excavated in the Late Neolithic cemetery at Kephala, and a settlement associated with it, in 1960–66. This is at present one of the most important Neolithic sites in the Cyclades, but it is badly eroded by the sea. Reports are included in the Ayia Irini excavations reports.

Since 1960, extensive excavation has been conducted at a prehistoric site on the promontory of Ayia Irini on the bay of Ayios Nikolaos on the northwest coast. It is an impotant site due to its proximity to the Greek mainland; and its deposits of Cycladic, Minoan, and Mycenaean pottery are helping to establish chronological relationships of these periods. A few pits had originally been dug by G. Welter (*AA* 1954, 47ff). The studies are conducted by J.L. Caskey and supported by the American School of Classical Studies and the University of Cincinnati, and have been continued into the 1970's.

The site was occupied as early as Late Neolithic times, and became of major importance during MM III. It was destroyed by the earthquake during LM IB/LH II, and reoccupied in Mycenaean times. An important find was a Mycenaean temple, with fragments of large terracotta statues; it was built in an early stage of the Middle Bronze Age and destroyed/rebuilt twice in Mycenaean times.

Published reports include: (*Archaeology* 16, 1963, 284ff; 23, 1970, 339ff) (*AJA* 71, 1967, 304ff; 72, 1968, 275ff; 73, 1969, 353ff; 74, 1970, 263; 75, 1971, 313ff).

Preliminary reports on the work were published as follows: (*Hesperia* 31, 1962, 263ff; 33, 1964, 314ff; 35, 1966, 363ff).

Final publications of material on excavations and explorations from 1966–70 were published by J.L. Caskey, titled "Investigations in Keos" as follows: ("Part I," *Hesperia* 40, 1971, 358ff; "Part II: A Conspectus of the Pottery," *Hesperia* 41, 1972, 375ff).

Since 1969, supplementary excavations have been carried out, these short notices appearing: (*AR* 1969–70, 24-25; 1970–71, 20ff).

Other major articles include: (J.L. Caskey, "Marble Figurines from Ayia Irini in Keos," *Hesperia* 40, 1971, 113ff) (Caskey, "The Early Bronze Age at Ayia Irini inKeos," *Archaeology* 23, 1970, 339ff). A full list of short notices on the island are given in *Hesperia* (40, 1971, 359, note 1; and 41, 1972, 357, note 2).

KEROS: The important Early Cycladic settlement and cemetery opposite the islet of Daskalio was originally excavated by Doumas in 1963 (*AD* 19, 1964, *Chr.* 409) and was further explored in 1967 and 1968 by Mrs. F. Zafeiropoulos (*AAA* 1, 1968, 97ff) (*AD* 23, 1968, *Chr.* 2, 381). Marble vases, idols, obsidian blades, and sherds were found.

Mrs. Zafeiropoulos also reported Early Cycladic settlements at Megalo Kastro and Gerani on Keros and prehistoric sherds and obsidian on Antikeros (*AD* 22, 1967, *Chr.* 2, 466).

Marble figurines of musicians in the National Museum in Athens probably come from disturbed graves opposite Daskalio (Renfrew, *Emergence*, 521).

KIMOLOS: The small islet of Ayios Andreas, off the southwest of Kimolos, was once joined to it, and in 1884 Bent noted house foundations in the shallow channel between the islet and Helleniki (Limni) (Bent, *Aegean Islands* 1885).

The cemetery connected with this settlement is at Helleniki (Limni) on Kimolos, and in 1944 was examined by Moustakas (*AM* 69-70, 1954–55, 153ff). In 1954 Kondoleon and Papadopoulos excavated Geometric, fifth century, and later tombs. Over 200 vases were recovered from 22 Geometric tombs (*AD* 20, 1965, *Chr.* 514ff) (*AD* 21, 1966, *Chr.* 380). In 1969, Mrs. F. Zafeiropoulos excavated 13 tombs of the 5th and 4th centuries on the shore at Limni close to the Geometric cemetery; Attic black-glaze and Late Corinthian painted vases were found (*AD* 25, 1970, *Chr.* 2, 423ff).

There is a site of the Classical period at Palaiokastro in the interior of Kimolos, which was also explored by Moustakas in 1936 (*AM* 69-70, 1954–5, 153ff).

KOUPHONISIA

Ano Kouphonisi: In 1969 and 1970, excavations were conducted by F. Zafeiropoulos at two Early Cycladic cemeteries, a small cemetery at Alonistria Chousouri with a nearby settlement, and a cemetery of 72 rock-cut graves at Agrilia. A figurine of Louros type was found in one grave (*AAA* 3, 1970, 48ff) (*AAA* 4, 1971, 214ff) (*AD* 25, 1970, *Chr.* 2, 428ff).

Kato Kouphonisi: Zafeiropoulos reported Early Cycladic settlements at Panaghia (though Renfrew, visting the site in 1963, noted only Hellenistic sherds), and an EC tomb at Nero, visited by Renfrew in 1970 (*AD* 22,

1967, *Chr.* 2, 466-7) (*AD* 25, *Chr.* 429ff) (Renfrew, *Emergence* 520-1).

KYTHNOS: Middle and possibly Late Cycladic sherds have been found at Ayia Irini to the south of the Bay of Loutra in the northeast of the island. It does not seem to have been an important site, but the cove to the east was a safe anchorage (Scholes, *BSA* 51, 1956, 12). It has also been reported that Kenneth Honea discovered a Mesolithic or Early Neolithic camp and cemetery at Maroula on the northeast coast of the island in 1972, in a study sponsored by Northern Illinois University. This site is unique in providing evidence of the earliest habitation in the Cyclades (*AJA* 78, 1974, note on 33; 79, 1975, 277ff). Apparently the Kythnos of the historic period was at Rigokastro in the northwest of the island.

MELOS: This island has been well known for the finds of important statues including the Aphrodite now in the Louvre, the Asclepius in the British Museum, and the Poseidon and Apollo in Athens. A great deal of plundering and unrecorded digging had preceded any systematic excavation.

In the area of ancient Melos (Klima, Plaka, Tripiti, Ayios Elias, Kastro), the British School under Cecil Smith, in a not very successful season during 1896, investigated the coastal area of Klima village and found remains of what may be ancient port installations. Further up the slope toward the acropolis, plundered Geometric tombs and remains of the Greek, Roman and Byzantine city were excavated (Cecil Smith, *AR* 1895–6, 347ff) (*BSA* 3, 1896–7, 35ff). On the smaller acropolis of Ayios Elias, in addition to sherds from the Geometric to Byzantine periods, Middle Cycladic sherds have been found (Scholes, *BSA* 51, 1956, 12) and Mackenzie noted sherds that he identified as 'Mycenaean' (*BSA* 3, 1896–7, 88).

C.C. Edgar excavated the Early Cycladic cemetery and settlement at Pelos (*BSA* 3, 1897, 35ff).

At Phylakopi, in the northeastern part of the island, one of the most important excavations in the Cyclades was conducted by the British School in 1896–99. The work was chiefly under the direction of Duncan Mackenzie, with Cecil Smith, R.C. Bosanquet, C. Clark, Hogarth, Edgar, E.B. Hoare and T.D. Atkinson. The site had previously been noted by Ross (*Reisen* 3, 13) and Dümmler (*AM* 11, 1886, 170). Three separate occupation levels were found corresponding to Early, Middle, and Late Cycladic; in the latter period both Minoan and Mycenaean pottery were found. The site was deserted by the end of LH IIIC. These important excavations gave the first basic insight into Cycladic civilization. The report of the excavations was made by T.D. Atkinson, F.W. Crawford, C.C. Edgar et al. (*Excavations at Phylakopi in Melos, JHS* Supplement 4, 1904). A further season of excavation was carried out in 1910 (R. Dawkins and J. Droop, *BSA* 17, 1910–11, 1ff). In 1974 excavations were resumed at Phylakopi by the British School, under Colin Renfrew, with the aim of further investigating the stratigraphy of the site.

Other sites south of Phylakopi are Kapari, a small site of the Phylakopi I period and later (Papadopoulos and F. Zafeiropoulos, *AD* 21, 1966, *Chr.* 2, 387); and Asprochorio, where damaged rock-cut tombs yielded Phylakopi I or II pots in 1964 (Renfrew, *Emergence,* 511-12).

Palaiokhori, ancient Zephiria, was occupied from the 8th century B.C. until 1793, when the survivors of an epidemic abandoned the site and moved to Kastro. No published excavations of the Classical city are known. In 1965 an EC settlement and a cemetery with four graves were discovered in the area (Papadopoulos and Zafeiropoulos, op.cit., 386-7); in 1966 two pit graves nearby produced Classical black-figure vases (*AD* 22, 1967, *Chr.* 2, 465). Another EC settlement was noted in 1964 at Stavros, southwest of the bay (Renfrew, *Emergence,* 512). On the south coast rock-cut tombs resembling Phylakopi I have been excavated at Spathi (*AD* 20, 1965, *Chr.* 513).

In the northwest, an EC settlement was examined by Mackenzie (*BSA* 3, 1897, 86) and an EC cemetery, probably associated with this settlement was excavated at Kalogries (Papadopoulos and Zafeiropoulos, *AD* 20, 1965, *Chr.* 508).

F. Zafeiropoulos reported a rock-cut tomb with 4th century BC vases in 1960 near Pollonia, and a pithos burial near Komia with 6th century vases (*BCH* 1960, 814). In 1969, N. Zafeiropoulos reported a pithos burial of the second half of the 6th century BC, between Adamas and Zephiria (*AD* 25, 1970, *Chr.* 2, 423).

Renfrew visited an LN site at Agrilia in 1963 (*Emergence,* 507). Finds from the obsidian quarries on Melos are due to be published in detail (ibid., 509) but for a discussion of the Neolithic Melian obsidian industry, see Renfrew et al., "Obsidian in the Aegean" (*BSA* 60, 1965, 225ff).

There is an interesting commentary by J.T. Bent, "On the Antiquities of Melos" (*Aegean Islands* 1885, 81ff).

MYKONOS: Little excavation has been done on Mykonos, primarily a stopping-off place for expeditions to Delos, and the topography is confused. Reports of archaeological exploration of the islands include: (Svoronos, *BCH* 17, 1893, 487ff) (Hans Möbius, *AM* 50, 1925, 37ff, translated and reprinted in Bent, *Aegean Islands,* reprint 1966, 505-11) (A.N. Oikonomides, 'In Search of Ancient Mykonos', concerning exploration in 1959, in Bent, *Aegean Islands,* reprint, 513ff) (Bakalakis, *BCH* 88, 1964, 555ff) (John S. Belmont and Colin Renfrew, 'Two Prehistoric Sites on Mykonos', *AJA* 68, 1964, 395ff) (H. Möbius, *AA* 1969, 11ff).

The modern town of Mykonos may cover the ancient town, though Oikonomides (op.cit., 514) feels that this site, with a not very good harbor, is one of the worst on the island. However, in building operations in the modern town, Mrs. M. Ervin discovered a magnificent 7th century amphora with relief scenes of the Trojan horse and the sack of Troy (*AJA* 67, 1963, 282-3) (*AD* 18, 1963, *Mel.* 37ff).

The Palaiokastro hill, south of Panormos Bay, has substantial traces of Archaic and Classical occupation on the summit, and evidence of Middle Cycladic occupation has been found on the south slope (Scholes, *BSA* 51, 1956, 12) (Oikonomides, op.cit., 521) (Bakalakis, op.cit., 556).

Oikonomides located remains of a settlement on 'Divouni' on the Kalaphatis peninsula on the south coast (op.cit., 519-20). He identified the two peaks, Divouni, with the ancient Dimaston. Sherds were noted from Cycladic through Roman times; Middle Cycladic walls were noted on the more northerly of the peaks; and two Roman shipwrecks were located in the harbor (cf. Bakalakis, op.cit., 555).

There are ancient remains in the area of Ornos Bay, the plain of Lino and the Piaty Gialos beach, including three towers. Hans Möbius identified all three as Hellenistic (*AM* 50, 1925, 39ff). The smallest of these, at 'Portes', has a diameter of 3.50 m, and a doorway 1.27 high, and Oikonomedes suggested this was a Mycenaean tomb. Möbius reconsidered the matter (*AA* 1969, 11ff) and concluded that there was no evidence for this view.

On Diakophti, the southwest spur of the island, near Ornos Bay, two plundered chamber tombs have long been known. (Scholes, *BSA* 51, 1956, 12) (Möbius, *AM* 50, 1925, 37f). They have been excavated by the Greek Archaeological Service, but the results have not been published (Oikonomides, op.cit., 517).

In the area known as Anavolousa, north of Diakophti, a scattering of pottery and obsidian was found on a marble ridge, probably of the Late Neolithic or Early Bronze Age (Belmont and Renfrew, op.cit., 397-8).

On the west side of the Bay of Panormos, the Mavrospilia rock forms a narrow acropolis. Erosion has left no traces of building, but numerous potsherds, obisdian, and a stone axe attest to Late Neolithic occupation (ibid., 395-6).

A surface scatter of Early Bronze Age sherds was noted at Bouka, in the northwest (Bakalakis, op.cit., fig. 17.1).

NAXOS: There are more than 35 EC sites known on Naxos (Renfrew, *Emergence,* 517ff). Tsountas excavated some Cycladic graves (*AE* 1898, 137ff), and in the first decade of this century K. Stephanos excavated hundreds of tombs and other remains on at least 19 sites (reports in *PAE,* 1904 through 1910). The complete contents were not published until 1962 by G. Papathanasopoulos (*AD* 17, 1961–2, *Mel.* 104ff). Among the sites are an EC fortified settlement at Spedos on the southeast coast (*PAE* 1910, 270) and a cist grave cemetery at Ormos Apollonos on the northeast coast (*PAE* 1908, 115).

Additional EC sites have been discovered in recent years. Among them are: Early Cycladic tombs at Akrotiri, northeast of Enkares (Doumas, *AD* 17, 1961–2, *Chr.* 272); 25 'Grotta-Pelos' type graves at Lakkoudes (ibid., 274); EC graves and building traces at Lionas (Avdheli) in the northeast (Doumas, *AD* 18, 1963, *Chr.* 275); at Ayioi Anagyroi in the Sangri area, a cemetery of 22 cist grave of the 'Grotta-Pelos' culture, and another cemetery of the 'Keros-Syros' culture (Doumas, *AD* 17, 1961–2, *Chr.* 272); a fortified EC site on Panormos, and EC graves which had been partly examined by Stephanos (Doumas, *AD* 19, 1964, *Chr.* 409ff); an EC settlement at Korphi t'Aroniou excavated by Doumas in 1963 (*AD* 20, 1965, *Mel.* 41ff); and an Early Cycladic settlement on the small acropolis Korphari ton Amygdalion on the coast, excavated by Mrs. Zafeiropoulos (*BCH* 91, 1967, 748).

South of Naxos town toward the sea southwest of the village of Tripodes, is the acropolis of Rizokastelia. There are abundant traces of occupation from prehistoric and later times. Stephanos visited the site (*PAE* 1910, 273) and Miss Scholes noted Middle Cycladic and Mycenaean material (*BSA* 51, 1956, 12). Early Cycladic occupation is not certain (Renfrew, *Emergence* 518).

In 1923 Dr. Welter and E. Buschor of the German Institute explored the Palati peninsula, connected to Naxos town by a causeway, and reported that the famous doorway belongs to the opisthodomos of an Archaic Ionic temple (*AM* 49, 1924, 17ff). Welter continued excavations at Palati in 1929 discovering sherds and other material from Neolithic to Late Mycenaean times (*AM* 54, 1929, 153ff).

Opposite Palati, on the coast, is the area known as Grotta, where Welter in 1930 found abundant evidence of prehistoric occupation. The area has been seriously eroded by the sea but is clearly an important site (*AA* 45, 1930, 132ff). North of the town is the Aplomata hill, where numerous Mycenaean chamber tombs were found. In a brief pre-war excavation, and since 1947, Kondoleon, Karouzos, and Zafeiropoulos have been working in the Grotta-Aplomata area and Naxos town. Material extends from Cycladic through Geometric times, Classical and later periods. Sherds of Minyan ware were found by the shore. Early and Late Mycenaean houses, a Mycenaean type megaron, and abundant Mycenaean pottery were excavated. The literature includes: (*PAE* 1939, 119ff; 1949, 112ff, and reports in subsequent years) (*Ergon* 1958, 165ff; 1959, 125ff; 1960, 185ff; 1961, 198ff; 1969, 141ff; and in subsequent years). Recent German work on the island is summarized (*AA* 1968, 693ff; 1970, 135ff; 1972, 319ff).

In addition to the Neolithic finds from the Palati peninsula, there is a Neolithic figurine in Naxos museum reportedly from Sangri village, and there are what are probably Neolithic finds from the cave Spilaio tou Za (Renfrew, *Emergence*, 509).

PAROS: Tsountas excavated Early Cycladic material at several sites on the island (*AE* 1898, 155ff). Among the more important are EC cemeteries and settlements at Avyssos in the southwest and at Pyrgos in the southeast; and EC cemeteries at Drios, Mnimoria, Galana Krimna, Glypha and Panagia. I.A. Varoucha excavated an EC cist grave cemetery at Ayios Nikolaos in the southwest in 1926 (*AE* 1926, 98ff). At Plastiras, about 3 km from Naousa on the bay in the north of the island, Doumas excavated EC tombs in 1962 (*AD* 18, 1963, *Chr.* 275).

Excavations have been conducted on and off in Paroikia (modern Paros town). In 1898 and 1899 Rubensohn and Hiller von Gärtringen of the German Institute excavated in this region and found a temenos of Asclepius near the sea, Archaic kouroi figures, temeni of Aphrodite and Eilethyia (*AM* 25, 1900, 1ff, 341ff) (*AM* 26, 1901, 157ff) (*AM* 27, 1902, 189ff). In 1917 Rubensohn excavated a settlement of EB III (perhaps going back to EB I) and the later Bronze Age (*AM* 42, 1917, 1ff). Welter visited the island in 1923 and recognized Archaic remains (*BCH* 47, 1923, 529), and Kondoleon explored the area in the late 1940's particularly the Elita section where he found inscriptions relating to Archilochus. Excavations at the settlement and cemetery in the Paroikia area continued in the 1960's under A. Orlandos, E. Stikas, and N. Zafeiropoulos. Material from prehistoric through Roman times has been found. Some of the more interesting finds concern Archilochus (*AD* 16, 1960–61, *Chr.* 245) (*AD* 18, 1963, *Chr.* 173) (*AD* 22, 1967, *Chr.* 463-4).

In 1969 D. Schilardi began a major topographical survey of Paros. Many new sites were noted, including a small Geometric or Archaic acropolis on the Oikonomos island in the Bay of Loggeris, east of Naousa (*AAA* 6, 1973, 260ff). Paros, in addition to having been the home of Archilochus, is noted for its marble quarries, in which unfinished statues still lie.

RHENEIA: As would be expected, since the island served as the necropolis for Delos, there are ancient cemeteries on the island, but most of the tombs have been plundered. In 1898, M. Stavropoulos of the Greek Archeological Society found the trench which contained the burials removed from Delos during its purification in 425 BC. The material found ranged from Mycenaean to Classical times (*AR* 1898–9, 326f). In 1923–24 Pippas excavated Geometric tombs within the same precinct. Rhomaios also dug at this time and found no later burials than 425 BC within the precinct, though burials outside the precinct continued through Hellenistic and Roman times. Reports by C. Dugas and C. Rhomaios have been published (*Les vases pré-helléniques et géometriques, Exploration archéologique de Délos*, vol. 15, 1934) (*AD* 12, 1929, 181ff).

In 1967, Siebert and Couilloud explored a cistern complex overlooking the Kato Guernale beach, indicating use towards the end of the 2nd century BC. Nearby, an apsidal construction and inscribed stelai were found, and further south, walls of Cyclopean construction (G. Siebert, *BCH* 92, 1968, 416ff).

SALIAGOS: This island situated between Paros and Antiparos, at one time probably formed part of an isthmus connecting the two larger islands. N. Zafeiropoulos first noticed the prehistoric settlement on Saliagos. For two seasons, 1964 and 1965, the British School, directed by J.D. Evans and Colin Renfrew, excavated on the island and have published a complete report (*Excavations at Saliagos near Antiparos*, BSA Supp. vol. no. 5, Oxford 1968). See also comments by J.E. Coleman (*AJA* 78, 1974, 333ff). Doumas was also involved in the work.

They uncovered three phases of Neolithic occupation, assigned to the early fourth millenium BC, and related to an early stage of the Late Neolithic period on the mainland. The deposits were well stratified, yielding characteristic uncomplicated pottery showing considerable uniformity. Much obsidian was found, and stone axes were common.

This is an important site and its interconnections with other Cycladic islands in the Neolithic period is discussed by Coleman (ibid.).

SCHINOUSA: F. Zafeiropoulos reports EC sherds (*AD* 22, 1967, *Chr.* 2, 466).

SIPHNOS: Most of the excavations on the island have been undertaken on the ancient acropolis at Kastro, on the east coast, east of the modern capital town of Apollonia. Dragatsis, who worked on the island from 1915, explored and planned the acropolis (*PAE* 1920, 147ff) (*PAE* 1922, 44ff). J. Brock and G. Macworth Young of the British School excavated from 1934 through 1937. The material extends from Early Cycladic through Archaic, Classical, Hellenistic, and later periods. Finds included a small quantity of EC and MC sherds, a Geometric house, and a votive deposit from a 7th century temple beneath the ruins of the Venetian fortress. Excavations were difficult, due to much medieval and later debris, and the area had been much disturbed (Brock and Macworth Young, *BSA* 44, 1949, 31ff) (cf. Scholes, *BSA* 51, 1956, 12).

Ayios Andreas, an important fortified settlement, was excavated by Tsountas in 1899 (*AE* 1899, 115ff). He found scant EC sherds but more of Mycenaean date. Tsountas compared the site to Chalandriani on Syros. In 1970, a Geometric settlement was dug here. Miss B. Philippaki re-examined the site in 1969, and concluded that a small settlement had existed in the Early and Middle Bronze Age. The fortifications appear to be Mycenaean in origin, but to have been repaired in Late Geometric times. The site remained occupied until the Hellenistic period (*AAA* 6, 1973, 93ff) (*AD* 25, 1970, *Chr.* 2, 231ff).

An EC settlement and cemetery is located at Akrotiraki. Tsountas excavated this cemetery and one at Vathy in 1899 (*AE* 1899, 73ff).

About 1½ km north of Vathy harbor, Mycenaean sherds and evidence of Late Mycenaean occupation are reported at To Froudhi tou Kalamitsiou (Scholes, op.cit., 12-13).

A notable feature of Siphnos is the large number of probably Hellenistic towers. Dragatsis in 1915 located 38 of them (*PAE* 1915, 96ff); J.H. Young more recently re-examined them (*AJA* 60, 1956, 51ff).

SYROS: In 1898, at Kastri near Chalandriani, Tsountas excavated several hundred Early Cycladic graves (*AE* 1899, 77ff) and an EC fortified stronghold and settlement (ibid., 115ff), which he compared to Ayios Andreas on Siphnos. Eva-Marie Bossert re-examined the site in 1962, and found considerable additonal material. The charcoal gave a C 14 date of 2580 ± 80 BC (*AD* 22, 1967, *Mel.* 53ff). Caskey dates this settlement to the EC III period (Caskey, *Essays in Memory of Karl Lehmann*, N.Y., 1964, 63ff).

Other sites include an EC cemetery at Pidima, and a cemetery at Ayios Loukas where 79 graves resembling those at Chalandriani were excavated. The use of this cemetery extended into the Middle Bronze Age (Tsountas, *AE* 1899, 79).

The ancient capital was located at the modern city of Ermoupolis, but the extent of the city and its industrialized areas makes excavation almost impossible.

TENOS: In 1901–3 Demoulin and Graindor, Belgian members of the French School, discovered the sanctuary of Poseidon and Amphitrite at Kioni, a short distance northwest along the coast from Tenos town (*BCH* 26, 1902, 420ff) (*BCH* 27, 1903, 233ff). Tenos town was the capital from the fifth or fourth century BC onwards. Graindor reports on the ancient remains from the town (*Museé Belge* 14, 1910, 234ff). In 1973 the French School under R. Etienne resumed excavation at the sanctuary. It appears that the site was also occupied in Hellenistic and Roman times.

The main center of the island prior to that time was at Xobourgo, directly north of Tenos town and near the village of Tripotamo. The site was noted by Kondoleon in 1938 (*AE* 1938–41, 1ff) and he resumed work at the site after the war, excavating from 1949–59 on behalf of the Archaeological Society. Prehistoric sherds were found, but the settlement flourished chiefly in the Geometric and Early Archaic periods. The excavations included a temple (probably a Thesmophorion), Archaic defense walls, and 6th and 5th century tombs. (*BCH* 74, 1950, 310-11) (*AR* 1952, 125) (*AR* 1953, 164) and reports in *PAE* for the years of excavation.

Another site at Akroterion Ourion (Vrykastro), located on the sea 2.5 km southeast of Tenos town, has been described by Scholes (*BSA* 51, 1956, 13). The site has not been excavated, but there is abundant evidence of Bronze Age and Geometric occupation, with emphasis on the Middle Cycladic Period, but perhaps going back to Early Cycladic. The MC and LC settlements were fortified.

At a site called Sparto, near Kardiani, the Italian School under Doro Levi excavated a Geometric necropolis in 1923 (*Ann.* 8–9, 137ff)(*Boll. d'Arte*, Aug. 1924, 83, 92-3). A Neolithic axe was found in a cave near Kardiani (*AM* 1895, 397).

THERA (SANTORINI) AND THERASIA: On the south coast of the small island of Therasia, a late Bronze Age town covered by volcanic ash was discovered on the Alafousos property in 1866. The site was partly excavated by Alafousos and Nomikos, a doctor from Thera, and continued in 1867 by Fouqué, whose book, (*Santorin et ses éruptions*, Paris, 1879) is a geological and archaeological survey of Thera and its adjoining islands, with a discussion of the eruptions of the volcano and a description of these early excavations. With Fouqué as a promoter, H. Gorceix and H. Mamet of the French School excavated the site from 1868–70 (H. Gorceix, *Descriptions. . .des fouilles effectuées à Santorin;* cf. *AJA* 9, 512). The Italian School excavated the classical site on the north of Therasia island in 1923, and near 'Kolombos' in the east (*Boll. d'Arte,* Aug. 1923, 83).

At about the same time the French School also discovered a prehistoric settlement on the north coast of the southwest peninsula of Thera itself, and did some digging at three points there, uncovering Late Bronze Age house remains (Fouqué, op.cit., 105-7). One hundred years later in 1957, S. Marinatos began his very important excavations at this site. In the first year, two Americans, Miss E. Ralph and J. Mavor brought prospecting equipment to determine the best place in which to dig. However, it was mainly by intuition that Marinatos began his trial trenches on the Bronos property, south of Akrotiri village. He was assisted by Emily Vermeule and N. Schlöbcke. The excavations have continued yearly since, and much Cycladic and Minoan material has been uncovered and reported in the press, both scholarly and popular. The beautiful frescoes uncovered are of prime importance. Marinatos hoped to uncover a 'Minoan' Pompeii below the layers of pumice and ash (pozzolana) and had been singularly successful in his goal until his tragic death in an accident on the site in 1974. The yearly results have been summarized in *AD, AAA* and *Ergon,* and in the series of monographs on the excavations (S. Marinatos, *Excavations at Thera 1-6,* Athens 1968–74).

Other Bronze Age remains on Thera include EC cist graves discovered beneath the pumice in quarries south of the town of Thera (*AA* 1930, 135). Zahn noted remains similar to the Akrotiri material in the river bed at Kamari (Hiller von Gärtringen, *Thera* 3, 39ff) and similar vases are reported from Akrotirion Koulomvon in the north (Scholes, *BSA* 51, 1956, 13). There is no evidence of Mycenaean occupation on the island.

From 1895 to 1903, largely at his own expense, Baron Dr. Hiller von Gärtringen of the German Institute, assisted by Zahn, Pfuhl and Dragendorff, excavated the ancient city of Thera, on the Mesavouno on the south coast near Kamari. Most of the remains are Hellenistic, for Thera was a naval base for the Ptolomies, but the site has been occupied since Archaic times. A complete Hellenistic and Roman city, with a theatre, temples, and underground water cisterns, was uncovered. In addition to yearly reports in *AM*, reports on the excavations are given in two books: (F. Hiller von Gärtringen, *Die archaische Kultur der Insel Thera,* Berlin, 1897) (*Thera, Untersuchungen, Vermessungen und Ausgraben in den Jahren 1895-1902,* Berlin, 1899–1909, 4 vols).

In 1961, N. Zafeiropoulos began excavating in the Mesavouno area, with particular emphasis on the graves on the northeast slope of the Sellada ridge. Much Archaic and later material has been found and excavation was continued through the 1960's into the early 1970's (*AD* 17, 1962, *Chr.* 268ff) (*Ergon* 1968, 93ff; 1969, 164ff; 1970, 161ff; 1971, 206ff; 1973, 97ff) and revelant years of *PAE*.

Eastern Crete
Nomos Lassithiou

ADROMYLOI SITIAS: Pendlebury records that Evans had found an LM III larnax burial at Adromyloi (*Arch.* 266).

Northeast of the village toward Sykia, at 'Ayioi Apostoloi', Platon in 1953–54 excavated a group of sub-Minoan or proto-Geometric and Geometric tholos tombs. He recovered about 200 vases, fibulae, pins, iron weapons, and Minoan sealstones (*KCh* 7, 1953, 490; 8, 1954, 511) (*PAE* 1954, 365ff). At 'Ayios Antonios' Platon found further proto-Geometric and Geometric tombs as well as two cemeteries of probably Classical or Hellenistic date which had been largely plundered over the years (*PAE* 1953, 296-7; 1954, 367) (*KCh* 7, 1953, 489-90).

At 'Pedhino', west of the village, Pendlebury noted traces of two circular tombs, possibly Early Minoan, and sherds of hand-made pottery (*Arch.* 290).

AKHLADIA SITIAS: In 1939 Platon excavated a well-preserved LM III tholos tomb which had been discovered by peasants at a place called 'Platyskinos' southeast of Akhladia. Among the finds were three pithoi. In 1952 he cleared the dromos. Nearby he noted remains of Minoan houses and he cleared an LM III potter's kiln. An extensive Classical settlement, going back to Geometric times, and Roman rock-cut shaft tombs were also noted in the vicinity (*AA* 1940, 304) (*KCh* 6, 1952, 476) (*PAE* 1952, 643ff).

In 1952 Platon also found and partially cleared an MM house at 'Riza' near Akhladia, and excavated it in 1959. It was part of a larger settlement and was probably built in MM III and destroyed, perhaps by earthquake, at the end of that period (*PAE* 1952, 646ff) (*Ergon* 1959, 142ff). (In *PAE* 1952 Riza is said to be southwest of the tholos tomb at Akhladia; in *Ergon* 1959 it is said to be northwest of the village).

AVGO IERAPETRAS: Arthur Evans had noted Minoan antiquities at Avgo in 1894 (*Arch.* 265). In 1901 the Americans Miss Boyd and Miss Wheeler excavated a Late Minoan building (*Transactions of the Dept. of Arch.*, Free Museum of Science and Art, Univ. of Penn., vol. 1, no. 1, 1904, 18ff). A hoard of bronze tools, rings, beads and seals was also found at Avgo (*AJA* 9, 1905, 277ff).

AYIA PHOTIA IERAPETRAS: In conjunction with the American excavations at Gournia, a short excavation was conducted in 1903 in rock shelters at Phermi, west of Ayia Photia, on the south coast. The shelters had served as burial places in sub-Neolithic, EM I–III periods (H. Boyd-Hawes et al., *Gournia*, 1908, 56) (*Transactions of the Dept. of Arch.*, Free Museum of Science and Art, Univ. of Penn. vol. 1, no. 3, 1905, 183ff).

At the same time, sub-Neolithic–EM II burials in rock shelters at Ayios Ioannis northwest of Ayia Photia were excavated (ibid., p. 214).

AYIA PHOTIA SITIAS: In this village east of Sitias, Davaras excavated an enormous cemetery of EM I–II tombs in 1971. Of the 252 tombs, the majority were primitive chamber tombs, and finds included abundant pottery (over 1800 vases of various types), stone vases, obsidian blades, bronze weapons and tools. One grave was found containing LM material (*AAA* 4, 1971, 392ff) (*AD* 1971, *Chr.*) (*Ergon* 1971, 256ff).

AYIOS NIKOLAOS MIRABELLOU: Ayios Nikolaos is the site of ancient Lato pros Kamara, the port of Lato. Spratt (*Travels* I, 142ff) described Classical remains, and Pendlebury noted stretches of walling south of the main port in 1934 (*Arch.* 353).

Xanthoudides reports an LM III kernos, a chance find in 1903 (*BSA* 12, 1905–6, 18). In 1951, an MM tomb was discovered with a small elliptical larnax, a small pithos, and a cup (*KCh* 5, 1951, 444). In 1953, a 2nd century BC grave was excavated by Platon, containing female figurines, perfume jars, and other vases (*KCh* 7, 1953, 486).

A proto-Geometric chamber tomb was excavated in 1958 at 'Sopata' (*KCh* 12, 1958, 477).

AYIOS STEPHANOS SITIAS: In 1954, proto-Geometric vases of a provincial character were found in a burial cave near here (*PAE* 1954, 368) (*KCh* 8, 1954, 512), and LM I vases were found near the village in 1958 (*BCH* 1959, 732) (*KCh* 12, 1958, 482).

AZOKERAMOS SITIAS: In 1962 an MM I idol was found on the Trao-stalos hill east of the village, and in 1963 Davaras excavated an MM I peak sanctuary consisting of a two-roomed building. Closer to the village Davaras excavated an MM IIIB–LM I building, perhaps an individual house (*KCh* 17, 1963, 405-6) (*AD* 19, 1964, *Chr.* 3, 442-3).

DICTAEAN CAVE: see Psychro

DREROS: The site of ancient Dreros occupies two peaks with a saddle between near Kastelli east of Neapolis Mirabellou. The Ayios Antonios hill, the more eastern of the peaks, was the ancient acropolis. Xanthou-dides excavated at the site in 1917, including a large megaron-shaped building and houses of the Geometric and Archaic periods (*AD* 4, 1918, *Par.* 23ff).

In 1932 the French School under Demargne began excavations. They located the ancient agora on the saddle between the peaks, and un-covered Geometric houses, fortification walls, and some Hellenistic walls. In a sounding on the acropolis hill they found an Archaic relief with a Gorgoneion (*BCH* 1933, 299). In 1935 Marinatos excavated at this spot, and uncovered a temple, built sometime before 750 BC, which he identified as the temple of Apollo Delphinios. Among the many finds were important Archaic stauettes made of hammered sheet-bronze (*BCH* 1936, 214ff).

In 1936 Demargne and van Effenterre of the French School again excavated at the site, particularly the area surrounding the temple. In addition to buildings of the Geometric period, they excavated a large Hellenistic cistern (*BCH* 1937, 5ff). They also excavated a necropolis of 25 sub-Minoan or Geometric cist graves (H. van Effenterre, *Nécropoles du Mirabello*, École française d'Athènes, *Études crétoises* vol. 8, Paris 1948, 15ff).

EPISKOPI IERAPETRAS: Over the years, several LM IIIA–B chamber tombs with larnax burials have been found in the vicinity of Episkopi. Several of the larnakes are finely painted (Xanthoudides, *AD* 6, 1920–1, *Par.* 157ff). (*AA* 1938, 471; 1942, 198) (*KCh* 1947, 838). The panels are illustrated in a book by Davaras (*Guide to Cretan Antiquities,* Noyes Press, 1976).

GOURNIA IERAPETRAS: Antiquities were noted here in 1900, and in 1901, 1903 and 1904 the American archaeologists Harriet Boyd, (later Mrs. H. Boyd Hawes), B.E. Williams, Edith Hall and Richard B. Seager excavated the site and others in the vicinity. The site dates from the EM period to Late Minoan times. There are some visible MM remains, but the existing remains of the palace and town date largely to LM I. There was some slight LM III reoccupation (H. Boyd Hawes, B.E. Williams et al., *Gournia, Vasiliki and other Prehistoric Sites on the Isthmus of Hierapetra,* The American Exploration Society, Free Museum of Science and Art, Philadelphia, 1908). In 1904 Mrs. Hawes found EM burials in three rock shelters along the Sphoungaras Ridge (*Trans. Dept. of Arch.,* Free Museum of Science and Art, Univ. of Penn. vol. 1, no. 3, 1905, 179ff). In 1910 Hall and Seager excavated the Sphoungaras Ridge, finding burials ranging from EM II to LM I. The EM II–III burials were simple interments in the earth. At one point the EM remains overlay a Neolithic deposit. Over 150 MM III–LM I pithos burials were excavated. The bodies had been placed in the pithoi doubled up and the pithoi were then inverted in the ground (E.H. Hall, *Sphoungaras,* University of Penn. Museum Anthropological Publications, vol. 3, no. 2, 1912).

For other sites in the Gournia area see: Kalokhorio (Vrokastro), Pakhyammos, Vasiliki.

IERAPETRA: The Roman ruins of ancient Ierapytna here have largely been destroyed, and there has been no systematic excavation. In 1860 a local resident excavated between the theatre and amphitheatre and discovered two marble sarcophagi which were taken to England by Spratt (*Travels* I, 253, 274). In 1931 Marinatos explored the Ierapetra area, investigating the remains of the ancient harbor and finding two headless statues. At Braimiana (perhaps Vaïnia) nearby he found small proto-Geometric tholos tombs (*AA* 1932, 176). The following year he found a Roman grave at Ierapetra (*AA* 1933, 314). In 1939 and 1940 a Neolithic female idol and sherds were found in the area (*EEKS* 3, 491ff; 4, 268ff).

Chance finds of Graeco-Roman remains including a statue and a tomb were made in 1958 (*KCh* 12, 411-12).

ITANOS: The site of Itanos, modern Erimopolis Sitias, in the extreme northeast of Crete,was visited by Spratt (*Travels*, I, 207ff) and Halbherr (*AJA* 11, 1896, 60l). Demargne visited the area in 1898 and copied inscriptions (*BCH* 1900, 238ff). Xanthoudides reported a tomb and two inscriptions found in 1919. One of the inscriptions concerns a conflict between Itanos and Ierapytna over the temple of Dictaean Zeus (possibly the temple on the site of Palaiokastro) (*AD* 6, 1920–1, *Par.* 162-63).

The French School, with H. Gallet de Santerre, A Dessenne, and J. Deshayes, excavated in 1950. In a necropolis which had been largely plundered they excavated some intact Hellenistic graves, and one grave which contained some Geometric sherds. On the east acropolis the pottery ranged from proto-Geometric to Hellenistic. The Geometric was particularly abundant, but the stratification was very disturbed. In the lower town fragments of a Minoan stone vase were found, and houses of probably Hellenistic date. To the south of Itanos a Minoan house with pottery of mostly LM IA date was excavated (*BCH* 1951, 190).

KALAMAFKI SITIAS: In 1942 an LM IIIB tholos tomb was found at Kalamafki, a village to the east of Praisos (*KCh* 1, 1947, 632). In 1952 Platon investigated an LM III site on the summit of a hill where it had been reported that figurines of the Karphi type had once been found. An LM III pithos and a small bronze axe were recovered (*KCh* 6, 1952, 481).

Pendlebury had reported sherds of Geometric to Classical date on the 'Kastellos' and Roman sherds at Sellia (*Arch.* 326, 343, 353, 375).

KALO KHORIO MIRABELLOU: In a short excavation in 1910 and a longer session in 1912, Hall and Seager excavated at Vrokastro, for the University of Pennsylvania Museum, a steep spur on the east side of the Kalo Khorio valley, which perhaps had served as a citadel for the entire area. The site had been occupied at least from MM times, but most remains of the rather poorly built town are of sub-Minoan to Geometric date. The site was a refuge settlement. Further Geometric house remains were found on hills to the south, and a number of tombs were excavated in the area: several LM III–sub-Minoan tholoi and chamber tombs, and twelve 'bone-enclosures' consisting of several irregular rooms of proto-Geometric—Geometric date (E.H. Hall, *Excavations in Eastern Crete, Vrokastro,* The University Museum Anthropological Publications, Univ. of Penn. vol. 3, no. 3, 1914, 79ff).

The same year, to the north of Kalo Khorio on the Priniatikos Pyrgos peninsula, an extensive Minoan settlement of EM–LM I date was identified, but it was much disturbed by a Roman deposit above. To the east of this, at 'Nisi', is a large Graeco-Roman site, possibly ancient Istron (ibid., 84).

In 1931 Marinatos found graves with Minoan vases in the Kalo Khorio area (*AA* 1932, 176). At 'Goula' Alexiou excavated an LM IIIB chamber tomb in 1963 (*KCh* 17, 1963, 405).

KANENE SITIAS (renamed Ayios Spiridon): From Kanene, near Praisos, LM III larnax burials have been reported (*KCh* 4, 1950, 534; *KCh* 5, 1951, 445). Platon excavated a group of LM IIIB–C chamber tombs at 'Ayios Nikolaos' (*PAE* 1960, 302).

KARPHI: see Tzermiadon

KATO ZAKROS: see Zakros

KAVOUSI IERAPETRAS: In 1900 Miss H.A. Boyd explored a number of sites in the Kavousi area, including a house and a group of four tholos tombs of sub-Minoan or proto-Geometric date on the 'Vronta' hill, southwest of Kavousi. One of the tombs was undisturbed and contained over forty vases. At 'Kastro' 13 rooms of a Geometric house were excavated, and a tholos tomb about one km to the southeast. Evans had recovered a number of Geometric vases from a tomb near here in 1899 (*Trans. Dept. of Arch.*, Free Museum of Science and Art, Univ. of Penn., vol. 1, no. 1, 1904, 13ff) (*AJA* 5, 1901, 124ff).

In 1951 Alexiou excavated an Archaic shrine at Kavousi which was in use at least from proto-Geometric times to the Classical period. It is similar to the shrine at Karphi (see Tzermiadon) (*KCh* 5, 1951, 442-3). Also in 1951, 23 Mycenaean vases (LM IIIB period) were recovered from a tomb at 'Xerambela' (*KCh* 5, 1951, 445). In 1954 9 vases were recovered from an LM tomb (*KCh* 8, 1954, 516).

KHAMEZI SITIAS: In 1903 Xanthoudides excavated a unique elliptical building of MM I date on the hill 'Souvloto Mouri' south of the village. The rooms of the house were arranged around a rectangular court. In addition to pottery and bronze tools, including two double axes, a hearth and fragments of an altar and offering table were found in one room, and figurines of the Petsofa type were found in rooms external to the main building. Xanthoudides also found remains of what is probably an LM III fort (*AE* 1906, 117ff) (cf. Mackenzie, *BSA* 14, 1907–8, 414ff). Platon suggested that the oval building was partly a shrine (*KCh* 5, 1951, 122ff). In 1972 Davaras re-examined the building, discovering a second entrance and determining that the shape was not entirely elliptical. Below the building he discovered three phases of EM walls, some of which were also curved and in places were followed by the later building. He concluded that the building was simply a house, not a sanctuary (*AAA* 5, 1972, 283ff) (Noack, *Ovalhaus und Palast in Kreta*, Leipzig 1928).

KOUPHONISI ISLAND: Spratt (*Travels* I, 243) describes the remains of the Roman town on the island, including three huge cisterns and part of an aqueduct. In 1903 Bosanquet and Currelly visited the island and found a great many MM sherds, a wall of a hut, and a complete MM jug near a large deposit of murex shells which had been broken to extract the purple dye (*BSA* 9, 1902–3, 276-7) (cf. *BSA* 40, 1939, 70ff).

KRITSA MIRABELLOU: In 1951 Platon excavated two LM rock-cut tombs near here, finding a large number of vases. Burnt human bones gave one of the first indications of cremation in LM times (*KCh* 5, 1951, 444) (*BCH* 1952, 242). In 1952 he excavated a small LM tholos tomb with its vault intact at 'Lakki' or 'Lagari' (*KCh* 6, 1952, 481). In 1953 he dug two proto-Geometric tombs in the area, discovering bronze ornaments, iron tools and vases (*KCh* 7, 1953, 485).

See separate listing for Lato (Goulas).

LAGOU LASSITHIOU: At Ayiou Georgiou Papoura above this village on the north side of the Lasithi plain is a very large site with material ranging from MM to Roman times, with Archaic material particularly abundant. The site had been noted by Taramelli (*Mon. Ant.* 9, 1899–1901, 409) and by Evans (*Academy*, July 10, 1896) (cf. *Arch.* 124, 291, 294, 324, 341, 351, 372). A Geometric tholos tomb was excavated near here by Pendlebury and M.B. Money-Coutts in 1937. They also excavated Archaic buildings at 'Itonadis', west of the village, and at 'Kolonna' and 'Kerasa' east of the village (*BSA* 36, 1935–6, 10) (cf. *Arch.* 361: Hellenistic graves at Kolonna noted by Evans).

LASITHI PLAIN: A survey of sites in the plain was made by H.W. and J.D.S. Pendlebury and M.B. Money-Coutts (*BSA* 36, 1935–6, 5ff; 38, 1937–8, 1ff). Pendlebury has also published a general discussion of the plain (*BSA* 37, 1936–7, 194ff). A survey has been conducted more recently by H.V. Watrous (*AAA* 7, 1974, 206ff).

For individual sites in the plain see: Lagou, Plati, Psychro, Tzermiadon.

LASTROS SITIAS: An LM IIIB grave was found at 'Langades' (*AA* 1938, 473) and an LM IIIB chamber tomb with an infant burial was excavated in 1959. The main LM III necropolis lay to the southwest of the town (*KCh* 13, 1959, 389).

LATO: The remains at Goulas, north of Kritsa Mirabellou were described by Spratt (*Travels* I, 129ff) and Halbherr (*Antiquary* 1893, 198) who first identified the site with 'Inland Lato' (Lato pros Kamara, its port, was at Ayios Nikolaos). Arthur Evans and J. L. Myres visited the site in 1894, 1895 and 1896, and they argued against this identification, believing that all the remains were prehistoric (*BSA* 2, 1895–6, 169ff). The French School partially excavated the site in 1899–1900 under Demargne (*BCH* 1901, 282ff; 1903, 206ff) and in 1910 under S. Reinach (*RA* 1913, 278ff) (cf. *BCH* 1929, 382ff). Inscriptions were found confirming the identification with Lato. The city was probably founded in the sub-Minoan period, but most of the remains are of the Archaic-Hellenistic periods. The agora and a temple in it of perhaps the late 7th century BC were cleared. The French School resumed work at Lato in 1965 and continued through 1971. They investigated the terraces around the temple where pottery ranged from 7th century to Hellenistic, the stairways and roads around the agora, part of the city wall, and Hellenistic houses (*BCH* 1966, 1125ff; 1967, 1044ff; 1968, 1124ff; 1969, 792ff, 1044ff; 1970, 567ff; 1971, 167ff, 515, 800ff; 1972, 567ff, 962ff).

MAGASAS SITIAS: In conjunction with the British excavation at Palaiokastro, Dawkins in 1905 excavated a Neolithic rock shelter west of Magasas village near Karydhi. It appeared to be partly enclosed with a wall in front. Much evidence of Neolithic inhabitation was found, including numerous stone axes, animal bones, obsidian chips, a millstone and 260 bone awls. Slightly to the west of the shelter a Neolithic rectangular house was excavated. More stone axes and millstones were found (*BSA* 11, 1904–5, 260ff) (Zois).

MARONIA SITIAS: An EM burial cave was discovered in 1936 (*AA* 1937, 224). In 1954 Platon excavated two EM burials caves with Vasiliki style pottery, two ivory seals and a gold bead (*PAE* 1954, 354-5).

MILATOS MIRABELLOU: The ancient town of Milatos, destroyed in the 3rd century BC, lay between the modern village and the sea. In 1898 Evans found a chamber tomb with two larnakes and about 20 LM IIIB vases (Evans, *Prehistoric Tombs of Cnossos*, 93ff) (*Archaeologia* 1906, 483ff). In 1919 Xanthoudides excavated two LM IIIB chamber tombs northwest of the village at 'Ayios Phanourios'. They contained painted larnakes and Mycenaean style pottery (*AD* 6, 1920–21, par. 54ff).

MOCHLOS SITIAS: In 1908 R.B. Seager excavated the islet of Mochlos for the American School of Classical Studies and the Boston Museum of Fine Art. In Minoan times the island was connected with the mainland. The settlement was most important in EM II–III. It was destroyed in the beginning of the MM period, though there probably continued to be a small settlement and the town was reoccupied in MM III–LM I. There is evidence of Roman occupation. Most important is the cemetery excavated by Seager. He excavated six large, rich EM II–III rectangular communal tombs or ossuaries in two sets of three, each set facing on a paved court, and 18 other small Early and Middle Minoan tombs. An enormous number and variety of very fine stone vases, fine gold jewelry, daggers, and pottery were found. The MM tombs were poorer. A series of MM III–LM I child burials in inverted pithoi were also excavated (*AJA* 13, 1909, 273ff: settlement) (R.B. Seager, *Explorations in the Island of Mochlos*, American School of Classical Studies, 1912: cemetery). Davaras also conducted research here (*Kadmos* 1973, 109ff).

In 1955 skindivers under J. Leatham and Platon explored the area between the island and the mainland. They noted remains of possibly Minoan walls and recovered an EM goblet. Roman fish tanks similar to those found at Chersonesos were also noted (*BSA* 1958–9, 273ff).

MOULIANA SITIAS: In 1903 Xanthoudides excavated two LM IIIB tholos tombs at 'Sellades'; in one there was evidence of both inhumation and cremation. He excavated another tholos tomb at 'Vourlia' nearby, where a villager had found tholos tombs 15 years previously. Remains of a contemporaneous settlement were noted between the two sites (*AE* 1904, 21ff) (*AJA* 9, 1905, 111-12). Traces of another tholos tomb were noted in 1959 (*KCh* 13, 1959, 389) and Faure noted evidence of LM III burials in the 'Kryphos Spilios' cave (*Fonctions*, 67).

MYRSINI SITIAS: In 1959 Platon excavated a cemetery of LM IIIB–C chamber tombs with larnakes on the Aspropilia hill. He also excavated, with Sakellarakis and Sapouna, a Minoan circular tomb at 'Galana Kharakia', the first tomb of this type to be identified in eastern Crete. EM III–MM I pottery was found, and about 25 larnakes and pithoi. At least 60 burials had been made in the tomb (*KCh* 13, 1959, 372ff).

MYRTOS IERAPETRAS: A Roman town on the site of Myrtos village had been noted by Mariani (*Mon. Ant.* 6, 1895, 321) and Xanthoudides (*AD* 2, 1916, *Par.* 28). Two important sites in the Myrtos area have been excavated by members of the British School of Archaeology: at 'Pyrgos', just east of the village; and at 'Fournou Korifi' or 'Troulli', three and a half km east of the village.

The EM settlement on the summit of 'Fournou Korifi' was noted in 1962 by Hood, Cadogan and Warren (*BSA* 1964, 95-6) and was excavated by Warren in 1967 and 1968, followed by two study sessions in 1969 and 1970. The settlement consists of a complex of more than ninety rooms, and does not seem to have been divided into individual dwelling units. Different areas appear to have served different functions; a kitchen area, a potter's workshop, and what was probably a shrine were excavated. The site was occupied almost exclusively in the EM II period, with two building phases. It was destroyed by fire about 2200 BC and not re-settled (Peter Warren, *Myrtos, An Early Bronze Age Settlement in Crete*, *BSA* Supplement no. 7, 1972).

In 1970, 1971 and 1973 Cadogan excavated the 'Pyrgos' site. The settlement on the slopes goes back at least to the EM III period, about 2200 BC. The summit was crowned with a villa in the MM III–LM I period, and the site was destroyed at the end of the LM I period. Volcanic material was found among the ruins of the building. The later Hellenistic building on the top of the hill was also excavated, and the Roman bath building on the outskirts of the village was explored and planned (*AR* 1970–71, 30-1; 1971–2, 24-5; 1973–4, 37ff).

OLOUS: Ancient Olous, the port of Dreros, lay at the junction of the Spinalonga peninsula with the mainland near the village of Elounda. The area is now occupied by salt-works and most of the ancient city is under water. The French School, under Bosanquet and van Effenterre, explored in the territory of ancient Olous in 1936–37. At Sta Lenika, between Ayios Nikolaos and Elounda, they excavated a 2nd century BC sanctuary of Ares and Aphrodite. Near Schisma they excavated a Hellenistic necropolis, and in an early Christian church on the site of the ancient city they found ancient inscriptions (*BCH* 1937, 473ff; 1938, 82). At 'Stous Traphous' they excavated over 50 LM III–sub-Minoan graves with larnax and pithos burials (H.van Effenterre, *Nécropoles du Mirabello*, École française d' Athènes, *Études crétoises*, vol. 8, Paris, 1948, 7ff).

In 1960, Orlandos further explored the early Christian church on the site of the ancient city (*PAE* 1960, 308ff).

PAKHYAMMOS IERAPETRAS: In 1914 R.B. Seager excavated a Minoan cemetery for the University of Pennsylvania. Some EM III child burials were found, and MM I, MM III and LM I burials in 213 pithoi and 6 larnakes (R.B. Seager, University of Pennsylvania, *University Museum Anthropological Publication*, vol. 7, no. 1, 1916).

At 'Alatsomouri' in 1951 Alexiou excavated an LM III chamber tomb. Numerous materials were found including two well-preserved and finely painted bath-shaped larnakes, and a lidded pyxis (*KCh* 5, 1951, 443; full report: *KCh* 8, 1954, 399ff).

In 1957 two MM burial pithoi were found (*KCh* 11, 1957, 339-40) and in 1963 Sakellerakis excavated an LM IIIB chamber tomb containing three larnakes, vases and sealstones at 'Kateri Koumos' (*KCh* 17, 1963, 405) (*AD* 19, 1964, *Chr.* 3, 440ff).

PALAIOKASTRO SITIAS: From 1902–6 the British School under Bosanquet, with R. Dawkins, M.N. Tod, W.H.L. Duckworth, C.T. Currelly, and J.L. Myres, excavated in the area of Palaiokastro, where Marshall had previously noted a larnax exposed by rain.

The chief site is at 'Roussolakkos', at the south side of the small bay east of the village. A large Minoan town built in blocks separated by streets was excavated. The site had been occupied since EM times, but most of the remains are of LM I date (*BSA* 8, 1901–2, 286ff; 9, 1902–3, 274ff; 10, 1903–4, 192ff; 11, 1904–5, 258ff; 12, 1905–6, 1ff; *BSA* Suppl. vol. 1, 1923: unpublished objects). Part of the site was later occupied by an Archaic temple of Zeus. It was mostly destroyed, but architectural fragments were found, along with various votive offerings, and a stele inscribed with a hymn to Dictaean Zeus, probably a 3rd century AD copy of an earlier hymn (published by Bosanquet, *BSA* 15, 1908–9, 339ff; also articles in same volume by Jane Harrison and Gilbert Murray). Cemeteries were also found at Roussolakkos, with EM II–III and MM I bone enclosures and ossuaries, and LM III larnax burials and chamber tombs (*BSA* 10, 216, 227ff).

Along the shore north of Roussolakkos is the 'Kastri' bluff, and about 1 km northeast of Kastri at 'Kouramenos' a group of buildings, possibly an LM III farmstead, was excavated in 1903. There were vestiges of sub-Minoan occupation (*BSA* 9, 329ff). Also in 1903, at 'Ayios Nikolaos', inland from Palaiokastro, a probably LM building, EM I cave burials and an LM I pithos burial were excavated. In 1903 J.L. Myres explored 'Petsofa', the highest peak on the cape south of Roussolakkos. An MM I peak sanctuary, with human and animal figurines, clay votive limbs and animal bones were found in layers of ash. There was also an LM I sanctuary (*BSA* 9, 356ff). Davaras excavated here in 1971, finding votive deposits (*Kadmos* 1972, 101ff).

In 1904 on the summit of Kastri poor LM III houses were found and at 'Ta Ellenika' on the south slopes, EM II–III and MM I ossuaries were excavated (*BSA* 10, 196ff; 11, 268ff). In 1905 at 'Sarandari', between Kastri and Roussolakkos, LM larnax burials were excavated (*BSA* 11, 191, 259ff). In 1906 LM II–III burial caves were excavated at 'Plako' on the cape east of Petsofa (*BSA* 12, 1ff). In 1905 the neolithic site at Magasas was excavated. See the separate entry for Magasas.

In 1962 L. Sackett and M. Popham carried out stratigraphical tests at Roussolakkos, Kastri, and outlying sites (preliminary reports: *BSA* 60, 1965, 248ff; *BSA* 65, 1970, 203ff). At 'Ayios Antonios' and 'Ellenika', LM III chamber tombs were excavated in 1958 (*KCh* 12, 1958, 482).

PETRAS SITIAS: In 1901 R.C. Bosanquet conducted trial diggings at this village east of Sitias. The site had been largely destroyed by modern terracing for cultivation, but part of a Minoan building and a great deal of Kamares style pottery were found (*BSA* 8, 1901–2, 282ff). In 1959 an LM III chamber tomb was excavated (*KCh* 13, 1959, 390) (*BCH* 1960, 822) (*AE* 1967, 84ff).

PISKOKEPHALO SITIAS: Evans had noted a Minoan site here in 1894 (*Arch.* 126) and in 1931 Marinatos found clay figurines of the Petsofa type (*AA* 1930, 176). In 1952 Platon excavated what had been the repository of an MM II–III shrine, finding many fragments of male and female figurines, and numerous terracotta rhinoceros beetles (*PAE* 1952, 630ff).

Also in 1952, at 'Berati' southwest of Piskokephalo, a collapsed burial cave of LM III, proto-Geometric, and Geometric date was excavated. A Minoan larnax and many Geometric vases were found and a fine terracotta fish (*PAE* 1952, 639ff). Another cave was discovered nearby in 1953 with ten burials (*PAE* 1953, 292ff).

At 'Kato Episkopi' southeast of Piskokephalo, an LM III tomb with larnakes was excavated. Nearby was a settlement of a later date (*PAE* 1952, 639).

PLATI: In 1913 near this village on the west side of the Lasithi plain, Dawkins excavated at 'Kato Kephala' northeast of the village, an LM I-III settlement. The chief remains are LM III, three blocks of building around a central court. The site was partially reoccupied in the Archaic period. At 'Skalia' he excavated an LM IIIB tholos tomb with a larnax burial (*BSA* 20, 1913–14, 1ff).

PRAISOS SITIAS: The site of ancient Praisos is spread out chiefly over three hills on the plateau between two streams which join to form the Sitia River, northeast of the village of Nea Praisos, formerly called Vavelus. Praisos was one of the chief post-Minoan settlements of the so-called Eteocretans.

In 1884 Halbherr visited the site and at the foot of the 'Altar Hill', which has been outside the city walls, found an inscription in Greek characters but a non-Greek language (*Museo Italiano* 2, 1888, 673). In 1894 he excavated briefly, hoping to find further inscriptions (*AJA* 9, 1894, 543; *AJA* n.s. 5, 1901, 371ff). In 1901 and 1904 the British School under R.C. Bosanquet with J.H. Marshall and R. Douglas Wells excavated the site, which appears to have been occupied more or less continuously from LM to Hellenistic times. Work was concentrated on the Altar Hill, where there had been a primitive altar. Votives going back to perhaps the 8th century were found, including miniature sets of armor, in the layer of ash. A longer 'Etoecretan' inscription of 17 lines and a fragment were found.

At 'Ayios Konstantinos' near the source of the eastern stream north of the village remains of a Classical temple were noted, and remains of a megalithic house. Various tombs of LM III date were excavated, and a cemetery of shaft graves which continued into the Hellenistic period. A

Hellenistic house was excavated in which was found an oil-press. At the north end of the plateau above the west stream the 'Skalais' cave was excavated. It was used for burials in the Neolithic or EM I period. Kamares ware and much proto-Geometric and Geometric pottery were also found in the cave (*BSA* 8, 1901–2, 231ff) (on the inscriptions: *BSA* 8, 1901–2, 125ff; *BSA* 10, 1903–4, 115ff; 16, 1909–10, 218ff).

In 1953 two tombs were excavated containing Orientalizing pottery and iron spearheads (*KCh* 7, 1953, 485). In 1960 in the 'Fotoulas' area Platon cleared an LM IIIC–sub-Minoan tholos tomb with bronze items, vases, and jewelry (*PAE* 1960, 303ff) (*Ergon* 1960, 212-13).

For other sites in the Praisos area see: Kalamafki, Kanene, Sklavi, and Toutouli.

PSEIRA: Seager excavated on this island in 1906–7, with B.H. Berry, finding a settlement occupied from EM to LM I times. There were later, Roman building on the island. He also excavated a cemetery of EM II–MM I burials. There were both rock-shelter burials and cist graves. Terracotta and stone vases were found (R.B. Seager, *Excavations on the Island of Pseira*, The University Museum Anthropological Publications, Univ. of Penn., vol. 3, no. 1, 1910).

In 1955 skindivers under J. Leatham, Hood and Platon explored the waters around the island. They noted remains of a Roman wall, probably a mole built across the cove (*BSA* 1958–9, 280).

PSYCHRO: Above Psychro village is the Psychro Cave, called by its excavators the Cave of Dictaean Zeus, although there is no firm evidence for this identification. (On the controversy concerning the location of the Dictaean Cave, see M. Guarducci, *Rivista di Filologia*, n.s. 18, 1940, 99ff; Faure, *Fonctions*, 94ff; Boardman, *The Cretan Collection in Oxford*, Oxford, 1961, 2ff).

Hazzidakis and Halbherr explored the accessible parts of the cave and the area around the mouth of the cave in 1886 (*Museo Italiano* 2, 1888, 905ff) and Evans visited it in 1885 and 1886. Among his finds was an offering table with Linear A inscriptions (*JHS* 17, 1897, 350ff). Demargne worked in the cave in 1898 (*BCH* 1902, 580-3) and in 1899 D.G. Hogarth investigated the cave more thoroughly, using explosives to move rocks and exploring a lower chamber where numerous bronze offerings were found, some imbedded in the stalagmites (*BSA* 6, 1899–1900, 94ff). The cave had been used as a shelter in the Neolithic period, and for burials in EM times. The cult in the cave dates from the MM period, continuing to the 6th century BC, though offerings were most numerous in MM III–LM I and the 8th–7th centuries. Pottery, bronze swords and knives, fibulae, rings, statuettes and double axes were found. Evans had never fully published his material. Boardman has now published all of Evans' finds, which are in Oxford, and representative finds from other excavations, and discusses the cave in relation to other early iron age sites (J. Boardman, op.cit.).

ROUSSA EKKLISIA SITIAS: A Minoan Bronze axe and a vase in the Herakleion museum are probably from this village southeast of Sitias (*Arch.* 249).

In 1939–40 the site of an Archaic temple was explored at 'Timios Stavros', 7th–6th century figurines and clay plaques were found (*EEKS* 3, 491ff; 4, 268ff). In 1954 more plaques were found, showing a goddess, warriors, griffins etc. and at 'Kastri', Platon discovered remains of a Greek city with towers and walls (*PAE* 1954, 364).

SITIA: Traces of a much disturbed MM III–LM I building, and an MM I burial cave have been reported by Platon (*PAE* 1953, 291-2). Xanthoudides reported an LM IIIB larnax from a grave at 'Papoures' found in 1903 (*AE* 1904, 52ff) (*AJA* 9, 1905, 112). Other LM III graves have been reported from the city (*PAE* 1953, 292) (*KCh* 7, 1953, 484-5; 11, 1957, 340; 12, 1958, 482) (*BCH* 1958, 778; 1959, 731).

South of Sitia a Minoan villa was noted by Mrs. Platon on the road to Piskokephalo, and excavated by Platon from 1952–54. The villa, of MM IIIB–LM I date, had been cut through by the road. Two long stairways ascend on either side of the façade (*PAE* 1952, 636ff; 1953, 288ff; 1954, 361ff).

Platon has worked extensively in the Sitia area. Finds are reported under individual sites, but his work around Sitia is also summarized (*PAE* 1953, 288ff; 1954, 201ff; 1955, 288ff).

SKLAVOI SITIAS: In 1963 Davaras excavated two LM III chamber tombs at a place called 'Pharmakokephalo' which belongs to an extensive cemetery plundered several years previously (*KCh* 17, 1963, 406) (*AD* 19, 1964, *Chr.* 3, 442-3).

SPHAKA SITIAS: At 'Keratidi' by this village near Tourloti, an LM III grave with fragments of a larnax was found in 1954 (*KCh* 8, 1954, 516). The larnax was later reassembled (*KCh* 13, 1959, 389).

SPHAKIA SITIAS: At Sphakia, southeast of Maronia, Platon examined an LM III tholos tomb in 1955. Nearby at 'Patela' he found a proto-Geometric tholos tomb with 15 burials. On the height above the tomb were traces of an MM III building which may have been a small peak sanctuary (*PAE* 1955, 294ff) (*Ergon* 1955, 101-2).

STRAVROKHORI SITIAS: In 1959 the place at 'Stoukipourou', where LM III graves with larnakes had previously been found, was examined (*KCh* 13, 1959, 391).

SYKIA SITIAS: At 'Kandemi Kephali' to the west of the village Platon excavated an LM III tomb with five burials. He also located remains of two LM I houses at 'Monasteraki' and 'Palaiotavernes' near Sykia (*PAE* 1954, 367-8).

TOURLOTI SITIAS: Seager had noted the existence of an extensive LM III cemetery here (*AJA* 13, 1909, 286), and in 1959 an LM III chamber tomb was excavated (*KCh* 13, 1959, 388).

TOURTOULOI SITIAS: (renamed Ayios Georgios 1958): In 1960 on the summit of Profitis Ilias, Platon excavated a large Minoan villa discovered by Phigetakis the previous year. It is of MM III–LM IA date. Finds included pithoi, vases, bronze tools and weapons (*Ergon* 1960, 208ff) (*PAE* 1960, 294ff) (*AD* 16, 1960, *Chr.* 259). Southwest of the village at 'Phlega' remains of a Minoan building were noted (*PAE* 1960, 302-3).

At 'Mandalia' EM graves had been discovered and in 1959 Graeco-Roman tombs were found (*KCh* 13, 1959, 389). C. Davaras has investigated a Geometric chamber tomb belonging to an extensive but largely plundered cemetery (*AD* 19, 1964, *Chr.* 3, 442).

TZERMIADON: In 1935–39 J.D.S. Pendlebury, assisted by Mrs. Pendlebury, Miss Money-Coutts and Miss Pascoe, explored the area of this town on the north side of the Lasithi plain, and excavated a number of sites (*BSA* 36, 1935–6, 10-11).

The Trapeza Cave was excavated in 1935 after having been discovered by Evans in 1896. It was thought to have been a shrine, but seems to have been used as a habitation in the Neolithic period and for burials in the EM and MM I periods (*BSA* 36, 1935–6, 13ff). Around the cave a Neolithic rock shelter, an MM I pithos burial and an LM III larnax burial were found in 1937 (*BSA* 38, 1937–8, 3). The Skaphidia Cave, used for Neolithic burials, and the 'Meskine' Cave, probably an MM I and MM III burial cave, were excavated in 1937 (*BSA* 38, 1937–8, 5).

'Kastellos', east of the village, was excavated in 1937. There had been an EM settlement which had been mostly destroyed by MM I and MM III buildings. Neolithic burials were found in rock shelters (*BSA* 38, 1937–8, 6ff).

The sub-Minoan refuge settlement on Karphi, the peak above Tzermiadon, was excavated in 1937–39. Over 150 rooms in the settlement and a temple were excavated. A number of female figurines with raised hands were found. Evans had excavated one sub-Minoan–proto-Geometric tholos at 'Ta Mnimata' and Dawkins excavated 17 more there and 4 at 'Atsividhero'. The finds from the Karphi settlement date from 1100–900 BC. The settlement was abandoned; the inhabitants perhaps moving down to the settlement at 'Ayiou Georgiou Papoura' near Lagou. The only later objects were Archaic and later figurines found in a sanctuary above the Vitzelovrysis spring and one object in a tomb (*BSA* 38, 1937–8, 57ff).

VAI SITIAS: The French School, under H. Gallet de Santerre, A. Dessenne, and J. Deshayes, excavated an LM I site at Vaï, about 2 km south of Eremopolis (Itanos) in 1950. The remains are perhaps of an isolated house (*BCH* 1951, 195ff).

VASILIKI SITIAS: On the 'Kephala' at Vasiliki, three km south of Gournia, an EM settlement was noted in 1903 and excavated in 1904 and 1906. A large EM IIB pre-Palatial villa and settlement were cleared, and the pottery, which has a mottled effect due to oxidization while firing, has given its name to the style 'Vasiliki ware'. There was evidence of an LM I inhabitation in one building (*Transactions of the Dept. of Arch.,* Free

Museum of Science and Art, Univ. of Penn., vol. I, no. 3, 1905, 207ff; vol. II, no. 2, 1907, 111ff).

In 1953 an LM III grave with a larnax was excavated at 'Selli' (*KCh* 7, 1953, 492).

In 1970 and 1972 Zois re-examined the Kephala site in connection with his projected publication of Seager's unpublished material. He found that at least a third of the villa may still be unexcavated; he found an EM II house and an MM IA house, and re-examined the LM I house. He also studied the MM burial enclosure which Seager had excavated but not published (*PAE* 1972, 274ff) (*Ergon* 1972, 113ff; 1974, 107ff).

VRAKHASSI MIRABELLOU: The French School under Demargne conducted a short excavation in 1929–30, finding a proto-Geometric–Geometric tholos tomb (*BCH* 1929, 328-9; 1931, 374ff). The pottery was reported by Marinatos (*AD* 14, 1931–2, 5ff).

VROKASTRO: See Kalo Khoria Mirabellou.

XEROKAMBOS SITIAS: The whole of the Xerokambos plain is littered with stones, traces of ancient walls. The pottery is entirely Graeco-Roman. This is perhaps the site of ancient Ampelos (Spratt, *Travels* I, 238) (Hogarth, *BSA* 7, 1900–01, 121). A peak sanctuary has been found in the area.

ZAKROS SITIAS: Ancient remains had been noted on the coast of Kato Zakro by Spratt (*Travels* I, 234) and they were visited and described by Halbherr (*Antiquary* 1892, 153), Mariani (*Mon. Ant.* 6, 298), and Evans (*Academy,* July 4, 1896). The site, which consists chiefly of two spurs and the valley between, was partially excavated by D.G. Hogarth of the British School in 1901. On the inland, western spur, he excavated two pits which contained Minoan pottery, including Kamares ware, without any stratification, and on the eastern spur he excavated remains of Minoan houses, finding pottery, traces of frescoes, and in one of the larger houses, hundreds of clay seal impressions and two inscribed tablets (*BSA* 7, 1900–01, 121ff).

In 1961 N. Platon reopened the excavation, with the support of the

Greek government and Mr. and Mrs. Leon Pomerance, in the hope of finding a palace. His excavations, which have continued to the present, have been important and successful. The palace, which had not been disturbed after its destruction and abandonment, was located in the depression between the two spurs, and it consisted of probably several hundred rooms, on two or three stories, and a number of annex buildings, which Hogarth's excavations had touched upon. Among the finds were Linear A tablets, and sacred vessels of various materials, including a rhyton with a relief scene of a peak sanctuary. A room containing a cistern with a surrounding colonnade is unique in Minoan architecture. There were remains of fresco decoration, largely destroyed by fire. Pieces of volcanic ash were found in the rubble, and there is no evidence of occupation after LM IB. The palace dates from about 1600–1450, LM IA–B. Remains of an earlier palace (MM III) were found in some areas, and also remains of an EM III–MM I buildings. Platon's excavations have been reported annually in *PAE* and *Ergon* since 1961. A book describing the site has been written by Platon (*Zakros, the Discovery of a Lost Palace of Ancient Crete,* 1971), and a more recent one in Greek (*Zakros,* 1974).

The surrounding area has also been investigated. Hogarth tested several sites in the Zakro valley and found traces of Minoan habitation, and burial caves in the gorge. In 1964–65, Sakellarakis excavated a Minoan villa between Ano and Kato Zakro of LM IA–B date, destroyed at the same time as the palace. Fragments of frescoes, a pithos with Linear A signs, and a wine-press were found. In 1967 two late pre-Palatial burial enclosures were excavated at Pezoules Kephalas on the road from Ano Zakro (see *PAE* and *Ergon* for the years cited). Numerous tombs of all Minoan periods have been found, particularly in the Zakro gorge (e.g. *PAE* 1962, 167ff; *PAE* 1963, 187ff).

ZIROS SITIAS: In 1963 Davaras excavated a small LM III tholos tomb. In addition to fragments of LM III larnakes and vases, Graeco-Roman sherds were found.

Southeast of Ziros on the top of the Plagia hill an MM I peak sanctuary was investigated. It was destroyed by the construction of a radar base (*KCh* 17, 1963, 406) (*AD* 19, 1964, *Chr.* 3, 442).

ZOU SITIAS: In 1954 Platon cleared a small burial cave, finding Geometric pottery, and nearby located a Minoan building which he excavated in 1955 and 1956. It proved to be a large villa of transitional MM IIIB–LM I date. A number of workrooms were excavated, and an oven which was perhaps a pottery kiln (*PAE* 1954, 363-4; 1955, 288ff; 1956, 232ff) (*Ergon* 1955, 99ff; 1956, 110ff).

East Central Crete
Nomos Irakliou

AMNISOS: In 1926, traces of a Minoan harbor and settlement were discovered about 7 km east of Herakleion. Marinatos identified this as Amnisos, a port of Knossos from which Idomeneus is said to have sailed to the Trojan War. Marinatos excavated here throughout the 1930's. Pottery from Early to Late Minoan was found in the harbor area. An MM III–LM I villa with frescoes of lilies was excavated, and a temple which showed continuity of cult from proto-Geometric to Roman times was found overlying a building of Minoan date. He also excavated a poros wall of Minoan date more than 40 m long (*AD* 11, 1927–9, 68ff) (*PAE* 1930, 94ff; 1932, 76ff; 1933, 93ff; 1934, 128ff; 1935, 196ff; 1936, 81ff; 1938, 130ff).

Platon reported that a square shrine chamber had existed in the Minoan villa (*AR* 1945–7, 118). Alexiou excavated at the site and determined that Minoan Amnisos extended west of Palaiochora hill, and that another settlement lay even further west. In 1967 various houses dated to MM III-LM III were excavated (*AD* 19, 1964, *Chr.* 3, 439ff) (*AD* 23, 1968, *Chr.* 2, 402ff).

ANAGYROI: In 1970 Miss Lembesi excavated an MM house where Evans had noted what he thought was an MM guard house (*P. of M.* II, 77) (*Ergon* 1970, 257) (*PAE* 1971, 28ff).

ANOPOLIS PEDIADOS: Proto-Geometric and Geometric vases were reported by Halbherr from the necropolis of Anopolis (*AJA* 1, 1897, 254, 258, 260, 263ff). An MM pithos burial was excavated by Hazzidakis in 1915 (*AD* 4, 1918, 58ff).

APESOKARI KAINOURGIOU: In 1942 German archaeologists excavated a Minoan circular tomb at this village in the Mesara and partially excavated a Minoan settlement. Finds included EM III and MM I stone and clay vases (A. Schörgendorfer, in F. Matz, *Forschungen auf Kreta 1942*, Berlin 1951, 13ff). In 1963 Davaras dug another circular tomb, with an ossuary and antechamber, of the MM I period. The tomb had been robbed, but stone and pottery vases and bronze and steatite double axes were found (*KCh* 17, 1963, 405) (*AD* 19, 1964, *Chr.* 3, 441).

At 'Ellenika' there is a large Graeco-Roman site. Pendlebury noted sherds and cistern in 1934 (*BSA* 33, 1932–3, 88).

APHRATI PEDIADOS: In 1893–94 Professor Halbherr in conjunction with the American Institute of Archaeology, explored the Ayios Ilias hill, noting terrace walls and Geometric sherds. He also excavated one sub-Minoan–Geometric tholos tomb (see under Panagia) (*AJA* 5, 1901, 393ff).

In 1924 D. Levi and the Italian School excavated ancient fortifications and houses on the hill, which he identified as the site of ancient Arkades. Numerous tombs were excavated on the western slopes, particularly cremation burials in pithoi. A great deal of Geometric and Early Orientalizing pottery was found, terracotta figurines, and various bronze finds. Inhumation burials were also found, and four proto-Geometric tholos tombs were excavated nearby (see also Panagia) (*Ann.* 10-12, 1927–9, 1ff).

In 1964 Alexiou obtained from a looted cemetery at 'Ailia' an Archaic bronze cuirass and a bronze mitra (*AD* 20, 1965, *Chr.* 3, 554). In 1968–69 Miss Lembesi excavated on the Hai-Zia hill and found Late Geometric sherds and bronze weapons in a building, possibly a shrine (*AD* 24, 1969, *Chr.* 2, 415ff) (*AD* 25, 1970, *Chr.* 2, 455ff).

ARKALOKHORI MONOFATSIOU: Hazzidakis partially explored a cave or rock-shelter on the Profitis Elias hill, which had been used as a Minoan shrine. He found EM vases and bronze weapons (*BSA* 19, 1912–13, 35ff). The cave had been much looted by villagers, but a chance find of further Minoan objects led to a thorough excavation in 1934 by Marinatos and Platon. The cave had been inhabited in sub-Neolithic and EM times, but the cult apparently dates from the MM IV period. Among the finds were bronze swords, some of them among the longest prehistoric European swords known, double axes, some in gold, and pottery. One gold axe was inscribed with characters similar to those on the Phaestos disc. Marinatos suggests that this was the Dictaean cave of Zeus (*AA* 1934, 252ff) (*PAE* 1935, 212ff) (S. Marinatos, "Zur Frage des Grotte von Arkalokhori," *Kadmos* 1, 1962, 87ff) (*Rivista di Filologia*, n.s. 12, 1934, 547ff) (cf. Faure, *Fonctions,* 160ff and passim).

In 1957 Geometric vases were found nearby at Pano Kalives (*AR* 1957, 20). Davaras excavated LM III tombs in the area at Tsoulouka Kolymbos and Xylangouri (*AD* 18, 1963, *Chr.* 2, 312) (*KCh* 17, 1963, 398).

ARKHANES: In 1922, Evans discovered remains of a large Minoan building and a large circular reservoir (*Antiquaries Journal* 2, 1922, 319ff) (*P. of M.* 1, 623; 2, 64ff). In 1935 Marinatos found proto-Geometric and Geometric graves in the area (*AA* 1936, 224). In 1948 Platon reported Minoan buildings (*KCh* 2, 1938, 582ff). In 1956, at Troullos, in the eastern quarter of the village, Marinatos examined a complex of MM and LM buildings; Platon excavated in 1957 (*KCh* 10, 1956, 40ff) (*KCh* 11, 1957, 329ff) (*KCh* 12, 1958, 467) (*Ergon* 1957, 82ff).

MM III and LM I–III buildings were excavated in the area by Miss Lembesi in 1970. A terracotta model of a Minoan house was discovered, as well as two Linear A tablets (*Ergon* 1970, 185). Other finds in the area of Arkhanes include a head of Athena and remains of a construction with water channels at Khoudetsi in 1952, and an LM IA building excavated by Platon at Xerikara southwest of Arkhanes in 1958 (*BCH* 77, 1953, 241; 83, 1959, 740).

Beginning in 1964, and continuing through 1972, I. Sakellarakis has carried out important excavations in the Minoan cemetery on the Phourni hill. Discoveries include three tholos tombs, which are among the very few certainly completely vaulted tholoi in Crete. In one tholos the unplundered burial of a priestess, queen, or princess was found (*ILN,* March 26, 1966). The third tholos, found in 1972, contained an EM III deposit of burials in 11 clay coffins, one pithos, and in the area between the coffins, gold ornaments and Cycladic-type figurines were found. He also excavated the associated burial structures finding much MM material, and a complex of seven shafts containing larnakes surrounded by a rectangular enclosure wall. He dates the complex to the 14th century BC. The Arkhanes cemetery is important for revealing tomb types which may be intermediate between other Cretan types and Mycenaean burials (*AD* 20, 1965, *Mel.,* 110ff; *AD* 21, 1966, *Chr.* 2, 411ff) (*Archaeology* 20, 1967, 276ff) (*Ergon* 1966, 135ff) (*Ergon* 1971, 237ff; 1972, 118ff) (*AAA* 5, 1972, 399ff) (*Kadmos* 4, 1965, 177ff) (cf. Branigan, *Tombs,* passim) (Sakellarakis, *Prähistorische Zeitschrift* 1970).

ASKI PEDIADOS: On a summit near Aski, east of Kastelli, Platon in 1956 noted a building with two rooms, possibly a peak sanctuary, near where an MM figurine of a worshipper had been found (*KCh* 10, 1956, 419-20) (*BCH* 81, 1957, 617).

ATHANATOI MALEVIZIOU: In 1957 Platon investigated two LM III tombs, finding a clay box-coffin decorated with papyrus in the shape of double axes, a silver ring, bronze razors and pottery (*KCh* 11, 1957, 335) (*BCH* 82, 1958, 791; 83, 1959, 740). More LM III larnakes were found in 1967 (*Ergon* 1967, 123-4).

AVDOU PEDIADOS: In 1898 and 1922 Xanthoudides explored at a place called 'Spiliaridia' about 3 km northeast of Avdou. A settlement site was found, inhabited in LM I, Geometric and Orientalizing periods, and four rock shelters with MM III–LM I burials. The material appears to be largely unpublished (*AE* 1907, 184, n. 166) (*BCH* 1922, 522) (cf. Faure, *Fonctions*, 68).

In 1937 Marinatos excavated a cave shrine at Ayia Phaneromeni south of Avdou. Material from LM I through Roman times was found, including offering-tables, bronze statuettes of worshippers, a gold double axe, Geometric statuettes and pottery, Hellenistic and later pottery, and lamps (*AA* 1937, 222-3) (*BCH* 1937, 139) (cf. Faure, *Fonctions*, 160) (Davaras, *BCH* 1969, 620ff).

AVLI PEDIADOS: Near Avli, south of Kastelli, building remains and LM I–II sherds were noted. A seventh century scarab was found at 'Mingilisi' nearby (*KCh* 11, 1957, 339) (*BCH* 82, 1958, 783).

AYIA IRINI: In 1906 Xanthoudides excavated two circular tombs at Ayia Irini in the Mesara, north of Koumasa. Material found dates from EM I–MM II (Xanthoudides, *VTM* 51ff).

AYIA MARINA MALEVIZIOU: At 'Stavromenos' near this village west of Herakleion, Hazzidakis excavated an MM chamber tomb (*AM* 38, 1913, 43ff) and at 'Kollyva Metochi' a sub-Minoan–proto-Geometric chamber tomb was excavated by Xanthoudides (*AD* 14, 1931-2, 1ff).

AYIA PELAGIA MALEVIZIOU: Evans noted an EM settlement here and LM III pottery from a cemetery at Kladisos (*P. of M.* I, 299). In 1962 Alexiou uncovered small LM I figurines, and in 1972 he excavated a settlement on the northern side of the bay, where Taramelli had reported Graeco-Roman sherds and walls (*Mon. Ant.* 9, 1899, 318). Alexiou discovered evidence of a lengthy Bronze Age occupation with pottery ranging from MM III or LM I to LM IIIC. The Minoan remains are overlaid with later occupation. Archaic and Classical pottery and Hellenistic houses were found. The site was thought to have been ancient Dion, but it may instead be Kytaion (*AAA* 5, 1972, 230ff).

AYIA TRIADHA: The site of Ayia Triadha was explored by Gerola and Savignoni of the Italian Mission in 1901, and trial pits were dug that uncovered Minoan buildings and material. Beginning in 1904, Halbherr of the Italian Mission made extensive investigations, uncovering more buildings. In 1911 he discovered a large deposit of inscribed tablets and an LM III shrine. He and others continued excavations in 1912 and found a large court near the palace, with EM and MM remains beneath it.

In 1934, the Italian School conducted restoration and conservation work at the site, and in 1938, L. Banti found an LM I floor in painted plaster, showing a sea-scene. In 1962 the Italian School made a trial excavation 100 m east of the Royal Villa and found Minoan figurines, a modest sanctuary, and votive statuettes of the Petsofa type. Also important were the Minoan circular tombs found.

In 1957, a group of houses at 'Patrikies' between Ayia Triada and Phaistos was examined; a collection of vases found to the east may, according to Levi, have indicated a potters' workshop. In 1959 another circular tomb at 'Gligori Korifi' near Kamilari, 1½ km south of the villa, was excavated.

The villa was probably built in MM III, became important in LM I times, and was reoccupied in LM III. In the Geometric period, it was probably a place of cult, and there was some occupation in Hellenistic and Roman times.

Bibliography includes: (Halbherr, *Memorie del R. Ist. Lombardo di Scienze* 21, 1905, 235ff) (*Mon. Ant.* 1903, 1ff; 14, 1904, 677ff) (*Rendiconti R. Acc. Lincei*, 11, 1902, 435ff; 12, 1903, 38ff; 13, 1905, 365ff; 14, 1906, 26ff) (*Ann.* 8-9, 1925–6, 71ff; 13-14, 1930–31, 147ff: the large circular tomb; 19-21, 1941–3, 1ff; 45-6, 1967–8, 7ff: Patrikies; 47-8, 1969–70, 407ff).

AYIES PARASKIES PEDIADOS: In 1934 at a place called 'Ayia Marina'

Platon excavated a proto-Geometric tholos tomb with numerous pithoi burials. Material found ranges from proto-Geometric to Orientalizing (*AE* 1945–7, 47ff).

AYIOS KYRILLOS KAINOURGIOU: In 1967 Sakellarakis excavated a plundered Minoan circular tomb at 'Akonaki' south of here in the Asterousia mountains. The finds are of EM II–MM I period (*AAA* 1, 1968, 50ff) (*Ergon* 1967, 116ff).

AYIOS MYRON MALEVIZIOU: An LM III chamber tomb with larnax burial was excavated in 1941 (*AA* 1942, 197). Beginning in 1966 Alexiou has investigated the Minoan necropolis at Vrysi here. In 1966 he found three sarcophogi and other burials in pithoi and larnakes to the MM period; in 1968 MM I burials, and in 1969 material from the phase between EM II and MM IA (*Ergon* 1967, 117-8; 1968, 140; 1969, 192-3) (*AD* 24, 1969, *Chr.* 2, 413).

AYIOS ONOUPHRIOS PYRGIOTISSIS: A collection of material including stone vases, jewelry, a bronze dagger and harpoon, sealstones and several Cycladic-style figurines now in the Herakleion museum is from this hill across the river north of Phaistos. It was described by Evans (*Cretan Pictographs, suppl.* 1895) and it is now thought that the material was looted from a circular tomb of Mesara type (cf. Branigan, *Tombs*, 1ff).

CHERSONESOS PEDIADOS: This ancient site, located west of the village of Limen Khersonisou, served as the harbor town of ancient Lyttos, and was important in Hellenistic, Roman and Byzantine times. The ancient remains have been described by Spratt (*Travels*, I, 105) and S. Xanthoudides (*AD* 4, 1918, *Par.* 30ff). Marble sculpture of the Flavian period was discovered in 1934 (*AA* 1935, 256). In 1955 a group of skindivers under Leatham and Hood, with the cooperation of Platon, studied and planned the submerged Roman harbor works; interesting rock-cut compartments, probably fish-tanks, were discovered (*AR* 1955, 35). (*BSA* 1958–9, 266ff). In 1956 Alexiou made a trial excavation of what might be a temple, finding inscriptions (*AR* 1956, 23 (*KCh* 10, 1956, 419).

DAMANIA MONOFATSIOU: An LM IIIB tomb with a rectangular chamber was excavated here by Xanthoudides in 1915 (*AD* 2, 1916, 171ff) (*AA* 1916, 156).

DHRAKONES (MESARA): In 1907 Xanthoudides excavated two circular Minoan tombs at this spot between the villages of Stavies and Phourno-pharango, about 3km east of Koumasa. Material found is probably of EM III–MM II date (Xanthoudides, *VTM*, 76ff).

EILEITHYA CAVE: This cave, south of Amnisos above the Karteros stream, is probably that mentioned in the Odyssey (XIX, 188). J. Hazzi-dakis conducted a brief excavation in 1886 (*Catalogue of the Herakleion Museum*, 1888, 13ff: in Greek)(Halbherr, *Antiquary*, 1893, 112). Marin-atos excavated in 1929, (*PAE* 1927, 27-8, 95ff; 1930, 91ff) and Faure visited the cave between 1953 and 1956 (*BCH* 1956, 96ff). Material ranging from Neolithic to Venetian was found, but the cult in the cave appears to be post-Minoan. It may earlier have served as a source of water (Faure, *Fonctions*, 55-6). House ruins with LM, proto-Geometric and proto-Corinthian sherds have been found in the neighborhood.

EPISKOPI PEDIADOS: LM III tombs had frequently been reported in the area of Episkopi: at Ta Markavousa (*AA* 1916, 156); at Tou Episkopi (*Mon. Ant.* 9, 1899, 368ff); at Christos (*AA* 1942, 196ff); at Ayios Apostolos (*AD* 15, 1933–5, 51ff); and at Kavousi (*AA* 1942, 197).

In 1951–52 and 1956 Platon excavated at several sites in the Episkopi area: LM III chamber tombs with larnax burials at Episkopi and Kalyvo-topos; a group of LM III tombs with double chambers and a small settle-ment at Kefala; and another group of LM III tombs near Stamni village north of Episkopi (*PAE* 1952, 619ff) (*KCh* 6, 1952, 472ff; 10, 1956, 419) (*AD* 17, 1961–2, *Chr.* 184).

ERGANOS PEDIADOS: In 1893–94 Halbherr explored the acropolis of Erganos, northeast of Aphrati, north of Xeniakos village. He excavated three tholos tombs, probably of LM IIIB date and noted remains of a settlement (*AJA* 5, 1901, 262ff; 302ff). At 'Atambachi' near Xeniakos, Alexiou explored graves, probably of LM date, in clefts in the rock (*KCh* 7, 1953, 491) (*BCH* 78, 1954, 156).

GALIA KAINOURGIOU: In 1963 Davaras excavated four LM IIIB tombs at 'Stavros' and a fourth neaby (*AD* 19, 1964, *Chr.* 3, 441).

GAZI MALEVIZIOU: In 1936 peasants found two Minoan terracotta female statuettes with raised arms, and a short excavation produced three more. The largest, 0.775 meters high, has a crown with poppy heads on it (*AA* 1936, 222ff) (Marinatos,*AE* 1937, 278ff).

In 1957 Alexiou recovered a clay box coffin from an LM tomb at 'Skafidhara' and found stone vases and two potters' wheels in a settlement nearby (*KCh* 11, 1957, 335). At 'Mikhanes' Platon examined MM burials in rock hollows and a Roman farmhouse nearby. In 1963 Alexiou excavated an MM III–LM I farmhouse at 'Ellinika' (*AD* 19, 1964, *Chr.* 3, 438) (*PAE* 1963, 201ff) and in 1965 investigated two burials in MM III sarcophagi (*KCh* 19, 1965, 282) (*Ergon* 1965, 141). More LM IIIB larnax burials were reported from Gazi in 1970. Several of the larnakes were decorated, one with a triangular-sailed ship (*PAE* 1970, 253-4).

GIOPHYRAKIA MALEVIZIOU: Northeast of the village a chamber tomb with three larnakes and LM IIIB pottery was excavated in 1959. Many other tombs were noted in the vicinity, and remains of the Graeco-Roman period (*KCh* 1959, 367) (*BCH* 1960, 849) (*AD* 15, 1933–5, 49ff).

GONIES: In 1954, a large Neolithic vase and a stone axe were discovered at Gonies, and in 1955 Platon found a possibly Neolithic building and an EM bronze knife (*BCH* 1956, 343) (*KCh* 1955, 567). In 1966 an EM–MM I shrine was excavated (*AD* 22, 1967, *Chr.* 2, 484-5). See also 'Sklavokambos.'

GORGOLAÏNI: In 1955, at 'Kastellos' nearby, what is probably a Minoan circular tomb, containing an EM vase, bones, and sherds, was discovered (*KCh* 9, 1955, 566).

GORTYN: The remains of Gortyn had been described by, among others, Spratt (*Travels* 2, 20ff) and the site was first excavated by Halbherr and

Comparetti in 1884–5 (*Mon. Ant.* 1, 1890, 1ff). Halbherr and Taramelli revisited the site in 1893–94 for the American Institute of Archaeology, explored the course of the aqueduct and copied inscriptions (*AJA* 1, 1897, 101ff, 159ff).

Further serious excavation began in 1909 by diverting a stream away from the Odeon where the Gortyn law code had been discovered. From 1911–13 Pernier and Oliverio worked at the site, clearing the Odeon, an Apollo temple, and various other sanctuaries (*Ann.* 1, 1914, 113ff; 2, 1916, 306ff; 8-9, 1925–6, 1ff).

From 1954–61 the Italian School under Levi excavated on the acropolis particularly, and an Archaic temple built on sub-Mycenaean foundations. A deposit of votive offerings stretched from the sub-Mycenaean to Roman times (G. Rizza and V. Scrinari, *Il Santuario sull' Acropoli di Gortina*, Monografie della Scuola Arch. di Atene, Rome 1968). Various other buildings in the vicinity were also excavated by the Italians (*Ann.* 30-32, 1952–4, 485ff; 33-4, 1955–6, 297ff; 35-6, 1957–8, 390ff).

In 1957 Platon excavated a large Graeco-Roman vaulted tomb at 'Palialona'. Many lamps and some vases were recovered, but the tomb had been plundered (*KCh* 1957, 334-5).

In 1957 Alexiou examined a room, evidently a Minoan shrine, at 'Kannia'. LM figurines of goddesses were found. D. Levi and the Italian School carried out further excavations in 1958 and determined that this room was part of an LM I–LM IIIB villa or factory. The building was destroyed by fire (*PAE* 1957, 148-9) (*Ergon* 1957, 82ff) (*Ann.* 35-6, 1957–8, 392-3).

In 1960–61, M. Michaelides and C. Davaras during excavation of an early Christian basilica, found an inscription mentioning Trajan. Many Roman graves were exposed during road building works (*KCh* 1960, 460) (*AD* 16, 1960, *Chr.* 256; *AD* 18, 1963, *Chr.* 2, 312). Borboudakis later continued excavations at the basilica.

In 1966 Alexiou excavated a complete proto-Geometric tholos tomb with about 50 vases, pithoi containing ashes, and a number of iron weapons (*Ergon* 1966, 152ff). Miss Lembesi reports on work carried out in Gortyn in 1971 (*PAE* 1971, 292ff).

GOURNES PEDIADOS: In 1915 Hazzidakis excavated EM tombs and LM III chamber tombs near the village (*AD* 4, 1918, 45ff, 63ff) (Zois, *Problems*).

GOUVES PEDIADOS: North of the village Davaras in 1963 excavated an

LM IIIB chamber tomb with three larnakes (*AD* 19, 1964, *Chr.* 3, 441ff) *KCh* 17, 1963, 405). About 500 m from the shore Miss Lembesi reported a 7th century BC cemetery of cremations (*AAA* 4, 1971, 384ff).

HERAKLEION AND SUBURBS: Though Herakleion itself was important chiefly in Roman and later times, the area of Herakleion has been occupied since the Neolithic period.

The chief Neolithic and Minoan finds have been made on the eastern side of the city in the suburbs of Poros and Katsamba along the Kairetos stream. In 1940 Platon had excavated a cave tomb of MM IIIB–LM I at Poros (*EEKS* 4, 270).

From 1953 through 1957, and in 1963–64, Alexiou has excavated at Katsamba and Poros. At Katsamba he discovered remains of what was a Minoan harbor of Knossos, including an LM III house with a shrine, and a bathroom and bathtub. Nearby was found a large MM house with fragments of frescoes which appears to have been destroyed near the end of MM IIIB. LM III buildings were found at a higher level. On the southern edge of this settlement Alexiou excavated an LM cemetery of rock-cut chamber tombs. Remains of Neolithic buildings and pottery were found among the tombs, and an extensive Neolithic settlement was identified on the hill above the cemetery. Alexiou excavated a large Neolithic house and a rock shelter with Neolithic burials (*PAE* 1953, 307ff; 1954, 369ff; 1955, 311ff) (*KCh* 1955, 558ff) (*AD* 20, 1965, *Chr.* 3, 551) (Alexiou, *Hysterominoikai Taphai Limenos Knosou*, Library of the Archaeological Society, 1967).

In Poros he examined remains of Minoan houses and cleared a votive deposit of MM IIIB–LM I pottery in a cave-like chamber (*KCh* 1959, 385). Miss Lembesi excavated two tombs in Poros, one of which had three rock-cut pillars supporting the roof. The tomb had been robbed, but MM IIIB–LM IA vases, remains of wooden biers, and gems were found. The other tomb was completely empty (*AAA* 1, 1968, 250ff).

West of Herakleion, Hazzidakis excavated an MM pithos burial in 1909 (*AR* 1909–10, 364). In the early 1950's Platon was instrumental in saving medieval monuments and in the restoration of the Venetian harbor fort.

In the Atsalenio suburb south of Herakleion, Platon excavated a Geometric chamber tomb in 1958, and Davaras discovered two more in 1963 (*AD* 18, 1963, *Chr.* 2, 311-12) (*BSA* 63, 1968, 133ff).

JUKTAS: In 1909 Evans explored a Minoan sanctuary on the northern peak of Mt. Juktas, the legendary burial place of Zeus. The sanctuary building is probably of LM construction. It overlies a stratum of ash containing MM I–II votive vases and figurines over the rock, and a reddish deposit of burnt earth containing MM III sherds. A massive temenos wall surrounds the peak, and the area was perhaps used as a refuge (Evans, *P. of M.* I, 151ff). In 1952, figurines of worshippers and animals were recovered during construction of a radio installation (*AR* 1952, 127). In 1974, excavations were undertaken by Miss Ioannidou.

KALANI VIANNOU: South of this village (southeast of Viannos) in 1966, Alexiou investigated tombs and pithos burials in the 'Phaphlangou' valley close to the sea where an MM III kernos and an LM IIIA kylix had been found. To the west on 'Trapeza' hill an MM IB–LM I settlement was found; and at 'Psari Phorada' to the east, a settlement which continued in use to LM IIIA (*AD* 22, 1967, *Chr.* 2, 487) (*Ergon* 1967, 118ff).

KALATHIANA (MESARA): Near this village, northwest of Gortyn, Xanthoudides excavated a Minoan circular tomb in 1908. The tomb was partly destroyed by villagers in about 1854, and numerous gold objects were said to have been found. Xanthoudides found a few dagger blades, bits of gold leaf and seals, probably of EM I–MM I period. The internal diameter of the tomb was more than 9 meters. He also excavated about 10 houses in the settlement to the north of the tholos, finding MM I–MM II sherds (Xanthoudides, *VTM* 81ff).

KALIVIA PYRGIOTISSIS: In 1958 Alexiou examined this area near the Minoan cemetery of Phaistos (q.v.) and traces of burials suggested that this may be the Classical and Hellenistic cemetery (*BCH* 1959, 747). At Kaliviana nearby, LM III chamber tombs were excavated by Marinatos (*BCH* 1925, 473).

KALOCHORAPHITIS PYRGIOTISSIS: In 1961 Davaras cleared an LM III chamber tomb, with two box-shaped larnakes and other burials, and vases including stirrup jars, a razor, and beads (*AD* 17, 1961–2, *Chr.* 286ff) (*KCh* 17, 1963, 385). Another tomb was found by chance in 1968 (*Ergon* 1968, 141).

KAMARES CAVE: The cave was first investigated by Taramelli in 1894. At least four LM IIIB–sub-Minoan tholos tombs were noted in the vicinity (*Mon. Ant.* 9, 1899, 291ff) (*AJA* 1901, 437ff) (J.L. Myres, *Proc. of the Society of Antiquaries* 15, 1895, 351ff: publication of pottery) (L. Mariani, *Mon. Ant.* 6, 1896, 333ff: publication of pottery). R.M. Dawkins of the British School re-examined the cave in 1913 and recovered further MM 'Kamares' ware. Occupied in Neolithic times, it served as a sacred cave in MM times (cf. Faure, *Fonctions*, 178ff).

KAMILARI (MESARA): The Italian School excavated two Minoan circular tombs at Kamilari near Phaistos in 1959. Tomb I has a number of antechambers. Material found dates from probably MM II–III (Levi, *Ann.* 39-40, 1961–2, 7ff). Branigan noted another tomb, largely destroyed, in 1966, with MM sherds (Branigan, *Tombs*, 170, no. 22).

In 1957 Alexiou examined a votive repository pit at 'Grigori Korfi', filled with terracotta figurines of seated goddesses with polos-crowns, and male and female worshippers carrying pigs or chests. What appeared to be a small temple was found nearby, possibly a shrine of Demeter. More figurines were found in the temple (*AR* 1957, 16) (*KCh* 1957, 335).

KANLI KASTELLI TEMENOUS (now known as **PROFITIS ILIAS):** Minoan, Geometric, and Roman remains cover a wide area in this region south of Mt. Juktas, and ancient Lykastos was situated in the vicinity. Evans noted sherds from EM I–LM I at Visala, east of the village, and a Geometric settlement to the northeast (*P. of M.* 2, 71) (*Mon. Ant.* 6, 1895, 233ff). Xanthoudides excavated a Geometric tomb at 'Riza' (*AD* 4, 1918, *Par.* 10).

Marinatos explored the area in 1949. In 1951 Alexiou investigated a rock hollow, 'Tikhida' toward Kyparissi. Sub-Neolithic–EM I vases, bronze knives, obsidian blades and ornaments were found, and EM I–II inhumation burials (*KCh* 5, 1951, 275ff).

In 1955 Marinatos began excavations in what he believes is the Minoan city of Lykastos at 'Vitsiles'. He uncovered the ruins of a large villa with MM II–proto-Geometric material, and a cave at 'tou Diakou ta Kellia' in which MM II–III, LM and proto-Geometric material was found (*Ergon* 1955, 104) (*PAE* 1955, 306ff) (*KCh* 1955, 559).

KAPETANIANA MONOFATSIOU: In1956 fragments of MM figurines were found near this village. In 1961 N. Platon and C. Davaras explored an MM III peak sanctuary north of Kophinà peak, finding some figurines of exceptionally large size (*BCH* 81, 1957, 617) (*KCh* 1956, 420) (*AD* 17, 1961–2, *Chr.* 287ff).

KASANOS PEDIADOS: Alexiou reported a cemetery near Kasanos. Larnakes and LM IIIB pottery were recovered from two tombs (*Ergon* 1971, 258ff) (*PAE* 1971, 284-5).

KATO SYME VIANNOU: East of Viannos, on the border of Lassithiou province, near Kato Syme, a sanctuary dedicated to Hermes and Aphrodite was uncovered by roadworks in 1972. Many Archaic bronzes were recovered. The sanctuary had declined in Classical times but revived in Hellenistic times, according to Miss A. Lembesi (*AAA* 6, 1973, 104ff) (*Ergon* 1972, 125ff; 1973, 118ff).

KAVROCHORI MALEVIZIOU: At 'Keramoutsi' near this village between Tylissos and Herakleion, Alexiou excavated an MM I sanctuary in 1966. Excavation was continued in1968, and the discovery of an unusual idol gave valuable chronological association with MM I pottery (*Ergon* 1966, 153ff) (*AD* 22, 1967, *Chr.* 2, 486) (*AR* 1968–9, 37).

KERATOKAMBOS VIANNOU: In 1957 on the coast south of Viannos, on the Kastri of Keratokambos, Platon investigated the acropolis of a previously unknown city which he had noted in 1939. Houses were excavated, from one of which came an Orientalizing pithos with relief decorations. A Classical cemetery had been located nearby (*BCH* 1958, 778) (*Ergon* 1957, 91) (*EEKS* 3, 1940, 498) (*KCh* 10, 1956, 420; 11, 1957, 332).

KHONDROS VIANNOU: From 1956–60 Platon excavated remains in the area of Khondros village south of Kato Viannos. On the Kefala hill he excavated an LM III settlement with extensive remains of houses. The settlement was destroyed by fire in the LM IIIB period (*PAE* 1957, 136ff;

1959, 197ff; 1960, 283ff) (*Ergon* 1957, 85ff; 1959, 134ff; 1960, 202ff). At the foot of this settlement at 'Rousses' he cleared a house-shrine of MM III–LM IA date, containing offering tables and debris from sacrifices (*PAE* 1957, 145ff; 1959, 207ff) (*Ergon* 1957, 89ff; 1959, 139ff).

Other remains in the area include an LM I–II settlement on the slopes at 'Tourkissa' (*PAE* 1960, 286ff) (*Ergon* 1960, 203ff) and an EM settlement at 'Boubouli' (*PAE* 1960, 289ff) (*Ergon* 1960, 205-6). A Hellenistic or Graeco-Roman circular tower or beacon was excavated on the heights at 'Roukouni Korfi' (*PAE* 1960, 290ff) (*Ergon* 1960, 206ff) (cf. *BSA* 1964, 81-2).

KHRISTOS ISLAND - PEDIADOS: In 1924–25 Mlle. Oulié of the French School excavated on this small island opposite Mallia, finding an MM I cemetery in the center of the island and a settlement nearby (*BCH* 1924, 497; 1925, 473-4).

KHRISTOS MONOFATSIOU (MESARA): At Khristos between the villages of Vasiliki and Krotos, Xanthoudides excavated a Minoan circular tomb in 1907. The material found is probably of MM I date. The Minoan settlement was identified on the Volakas hill above the tomb (Xanthoudides, *VTM*, 70ff). Evan noted an MM peak sanctuary (*P. of M.* 2, 81).

KNOSSOS: It was long known that there were antiquities on this site, but it was not until the private excavation of M. Kalokairinos in 1877 followed by Haussoullier and Stillman in 1880, and Fabricius in 1886 (*AM* 11, 1886, 110ff) that it was realized that this was an important site. Schliemann attempted to purchase the property, but was not successful. The excavations begun by Sir Arthur Evans in 1899 revealed a civilization he termed Minoan, which became world famous. Evans was assisted at various times, by D. Mackenzie, Hogarth, Fyfe, Hutchinson, Piet de Jong, Desborough, Dunbabin, Blakeway and Payne. After Evans' death in 1941 the excavations were continued by the British School, after 1951 under M.S.F. Hood, and recently under M.R. Popham and L.H. Sackett. Others who have assisted in the excavation at various times include: J. Boardman, J.M. Cook, G.L. Huxley, J.Lazenby, J.N. Coldstream, J.D. Evans, E. Jones, A. Snodgrass, G. Cadogan and Mrs. D. French. The site, most famous for the Minoan palace, town and cemeteries, was occupied throughout antiquity from about 6000 BC.

The Minoan remains are built on a large Neolithic tell. The post-

Minoan city was one of the major cities of the island, though the site of the palace itself was not reoccupied except by a temple. The results of excavations since 1899 have appeared in enormous quantities in both the scholarly and popular press. Of the two standard works, one is by Evans (*The Palace of Minos*, 4 vols. plus index volume, 1921–35) and the other is by Pendlebury (*A Handbook to the Palace of Minos, Knossos*, 1954). Reports since 1940 have been published frequently, at times annually, in *BSA* and in *AR*. Neolithic remains are covered by J.D. Evans (*BSA* 59, 1964; 63, 1968) and post-Minoan remains are published (*BSA* 56, 1961; 57, 1962). There is also the book by J.N. Coldstream (*Knossos, the Sanctuary of Demeter, BSA* Suppl. no. 8, London 1973).

KOMO PYRGIOTISSIS: Evans (*P. of M.*, 88) describes the remains of a Minoan port at this site just north of Matala. Evans noted sherds of most Minoan periods except LM III, and also found Geometric sherds and a large LM I building. Neolithic sherds have been reported (Pendlebury, *Arch. 45*).

KOUMASA (MESARA): In 1904–6 Dr. S. Xanthoudides excavated one square and three circular tombs at Koumasa, about 10 km southeast of Gortyn. Material from the circular graves indicates that they were in use from EM I through at least MM I. Tombs B and E are among the larger of the circular tombs in the Mesara, both have internal diameters of over 9 meters (Xanthoudides, *VTM* 3ff). Xanthoudides conducted trial excavations in the settlement connected with these tombs on the 'Korakies' hill, finding mainly Middle and Late Minoan material in houses (ibid., 49-50). See also nearby sites under 'Ayia Irini', 'Porti', 'Khristos', and 'Koutsokera'.

KOUNAVI PEDIADOS: Near Kounavi, at the site of ancient Eltyna, Xanthoudides excavated a Doric temple at 'Zagourianoi' (*AD* 4, 1918, *Par.* 24-5) and in 1956 Platon investigated large blocks of squared masonry indicating a public building or temple (*KCh* 1956, 418-9).

KOURTES: At Kourtes, north of Gortyn, 3 proto-Geometric–Geometric tombs were explored by Halbherr and Taramelli in 1893–94 (*AJA* 5, 1901, 287ff, 294ff, 305ff).

KOUSES KAINOURGIOU: In 1925–26 Marinatos excavated an MM II–LM I house at a place called 'Tou Brachnou O Lakkos' near this village south of Phaistos. He found pithoi and stone vessels in the house and also excavated LM III burials (*AD* 9, 1924, 53ff).

KOUTSOKERA (MESARA): In 1907 north of Vasiliki village, Xanthoudides excavated a circular Minoan tomb in which was found EM I–II material. 100 m to the south at a place called 'Salame' he excavated a similar tomb and located the settlement with which it was connected only about 10 m away. Middle and Late Minoan sherds were found in the house (Xanthoudides, *VTM* 73ff).

KRASI PEDIADOS: In 1929 Marinatos excavated an EM circular tomb previously noted by Evans in 1926. Sub-Neolithic–EM I vases were found by the tomb and deposits in the tomb range from EM II–MM I. This is the only EM I tomb of Mesara type known outside the Mesara (*AD* 12, 1929, 102ff).

Other Minoan graves are known in the vicinity (*KCh* 13, 1959, 386-7) (cf. Branigan, *Tombs* 4, 142ff). Buildings with MM III–LM I sherds were excavated in the vicinity by Alexiou in 1963 (*AD* 19, 1964, *Chr.* 440).

KYPARISSI TEMENOUS: See Kanli Kastelli for EM burials in 'Tikhida' rock shelter.

LEBENA: The precinct of Asclepios in this town (modern Lendas), the ancient port of Gortyn, was excavated by Halbherr and Piginoni of the Italian Mission in 1900 (*Rendiconti dell'Acc. Lincei,* 1901, 300ff). A temple, fountain and baths were found. In 1958–60, Alexiou excavated Minoan circular tombs in the area, at 'Papoura', 'Yerokambos', and 'Zervou'. This is an important site, as much material was found, confirming trade with Egypt and the Cyclades. One tomb had burials going back as far as sub-Neolithic, but most of the material found was EM II–MM II, with no EM III interface (*AD* 16, 1960, *Chr.* 257-8) (Alexiou, *ILN,* Aug. 6, 1960) (*BCH* 83, 1959, 742ff; 85, 1961, 886ff) (cf. Branigan, *Tombs,* passim) (*KCh* 12, 1958, 470ff; 13, 1959, 370ff; 14, 1960, 510; 15-16, 1961–2, 88ff). In 1971, Alexiou noted the discovery of a Roman cemetery during road building operations (*Ergon* 1971, 261-2).

LIGORTYNO MONOFATSIOU: Sir Arthur Evans dug an LM III tholos tomb near here (Evans, *Diary* 8/5/94) and several LM IIIA–B chamber tombs with larnax burials have been excavated in the vicinity (Taramelli, *Mon. Ant.* 9, 1899, 423; 14, 1904, 656ff) (*BCH* 1907, 116).

Wace and Blegen noted an extensive proto-Geometric and Geometric settlement on the south slope of Kephala, east of the village (*BSA* 33, 1932–3, 85) and in 1961 Miss Papadaki excavated a Geometric chamber tomb (*AD* 17, 1961–2, *Chr.* 284ff). Vases were published (*CVA Louvre*).

LYTTOS: The Roman remains of the city of Lyttos, near Aski, are described by Spratt (*Travels* 1, 94) and Taramelli (*Mon. Ant.* 9, 1899, 387). In 1952 a Late Roman tomb was discovered; rings and other jewelry were found (*AR* 1952, 128). In 1953 Platon and Levi explored the site, and in 1955 and 1957 in the 'Anemomyloi' area Platon excavated an Archaic house, finding interesting relief pithoi (*KCh* 1955, 567; 1957, 336). In 1968 Miss Lembesi reported finding fragments of Archaic pithoi (*AD* 24, 1969, *Chr.* 2, 418).

MALATHRES PEDIADOS: Platon and Miss K. Mavriyannaki explored an LM III tomb with a larnax and several other tombs at Malathres in the Pediados district (*AD* 17, 1961-2, *Chr.* 284) (*KCh* 17, 1963, 385). An LM III chamber tomb had previously been reported here (*KCh* 5, 1951, 445) (*BCH* 76, 1952, 240).

MALLIA: In 1915 and 1919 the site of the palace was partially excavated by Hazzidakis (*PAE* 1915, 108ff; 1919, 50ff) (*AD* 4, 1918, *Par.* 12ff). In 1921 the French School, with M.L. Renaudin as its Secretary, became involved with the site; excavations continued almost every year until the late 1930's and began again in 1945, and are still going on. In the late 1920's, the work was conducted under Joly, Flaceliére, with Chapouthier and Demargne continuing the work into the 1930's. Those involved after World War II include Chapouthier, Gallet de Santerre, Deshayes, Dessenne, van Effenterre, Pelon, and Poursat.

Middle Minoan finds have been most interesting; the first palace dates to MM I, and the second to MM II–LM I. In addition to the palace, a series of large houses were excavated, mostly of MM III–LM I date, an underground crypt or court, a building possibly for public meetings west of the palace (H. van Effenterre, *Revue Historique* 1963, 1ff), a building southwest of the palace with horns of consecration, and a seal-maker's workshop. North of the palace are the Minoan cemeteries including at 'Khrysolakkos', about 455 m north of the palace, a large, rich burial enclosure from which the 'Aegean treasure' in the British Museum may have come (Demargne, *Études Crétoises* 7, 1945, 25ff) (*BSA* 52, 1957, 42ff). On the coast, caves were used as ossuaries in the EM III period (*BCH* 1929, 527). There was previous Neolithic occupation on the site, and in 'Anavochlos' nearby, Geometric and Archaic walls, tombs, and sherds came to light in 1929.

The excavations have been described yearly in *BCH* and monographs on all aspects of the site have been published by École française d'Athènes, Paris (*Études Crétoises*, vols. 1-2, 4-7, 9, 11-13, 16-19, 1928–74). Excavations have also been reported annually in *AD, Chr.* in recent years.

MARATHOKEPHALO KAINOURGIOU (MESARA): In 1917 Xanthoudides excavated two circular tombs at Marathokephalo between the villages of Panagia and Moroni, northwest of Gortyn. The material found ranges from probably EM I through MM I (*AD* 4, 1918, *Par.* 15ff).

MATALA PYRGIOTISSIS: Spratt (*Travels* 2, 21) noted that Roman remains at Matala and Roman tombs have been excavated (*Rendiconti dell' Accademia Lincei*, 1907, 299) (*Ergon*, 1969, 195) (*PAE* 1969, 246ff).

MATHIA PEDIADOS: At 'Stavroplaka' near Mathia, southeast of Kastelli, Platon excavated three MM pithos burials in a cleft in the rock in 1957. Northwest of Mathia at 'Katalimmata', a house with LM III pithoi was investigated and nearby substantial remains of a settlement, apparently LM I, were noted. A Roman farmhouse was later built on the site (*BCH* 82, 1958, 783) (*KCh* 1957, 334).

MELESES PEDIADOS: In 1955, at a spot near 'Pateles', an LM III shaft-grave was found containing two sarcophagi (*KCh* 1955, 566).

MESARA: The numerous sites in this region are listed separately except for those grouped under 'Moni Odegetrias', in the western Asterousian Mountains. The basic works on the Mesara tombs are by S. Xanthoudides (*The Vaulted Tombs of Mesara*, London 1924) and K. Branigan (*The Tombs of Mesara*, London 1970). Following Branigan, the term 'tholos' has been avoided in the description of these sites. For Cretan tombs in general and bibliography see Ingo Pini (*Beiträge zur minoischen Gräberkunde*, Deutsches Archäologisches Institut, Wiesbaden, 1968).

MIAMOU KAINOURGIOU: Under the auspices of the American Institute of Archaeology in 1894, Taramelli excavated a Neolithic–EM I cave here, finding vases and sherds, and indication of habitation and EM I inhumation burials (*AJA* 1, 1897, 287ff) (cf. Faure, *Fonctions*, 52-3) (*KCh* 1951, 290-91).

MONI MALEVIZIOU: On a hill southwest of Moni, Platon cleared an LM chamber tomb containing box-shaped larnakes in 1958 (*KCh* 1958, 467).

MONI ODEGETRIAS KAINOURGIOU: Several sites have been explored in this region in the western section of the Asterousian Mountains, and it appears that this area had a considerable population in the EM period (*AR* 1968–9, 37). In 1966 Alexiou cleared two well-preserved but plundered circular tombs in use from EM I to MM I; he also examined the associated settlement. Other circular tombs were found along the coast at Agiopharangou, Kaloi Limenes, Lenda, the ancient Lebena (q.v.), and Trypiti (q.v.) by Alexiou and Davaras. In 1967 an LM III settlement was found at Vathi north of Kephali and the site of Hellenistic and Roman Lasaia was located east of Kaloi Limenes (*AD* 18, 1963, *Chr.* 2, 312; *AD* 20, 1965, *Chr.* 3, 562ff; *AD* 22, 1967, *Chr.* 2, 482ff; *AD* 23, 1968, *Chr.* 2, 405).

In 1971, D.J. Blackman and K. Branigan conducted a thorough survey of the Agiopharango gorge from Moni Odegetrias to the coast. The gorge was most intensively occupied in the Early Bronze Age, the Hellenistic and Roman periods, and the Late Byzantine and Venetian times. Fifteen EM I–MM I sites were noted, including eight circular tombs (including those previously excavated by Alexiou). Eight MM I–LM III sites were recorded including two or possibly three peak sanctuaries. The period from proto-Geometric to the late fifth century appears to be a total blank. Most of the Hellenistic and Roman sites were farmsteads, though there was one settlement of considerable size dating from the late 5th or early 4th century to the first century BC. Blackman and Branigan also surveyed the south coast from the mouth of the gorge to ancient Lasaia and the Graeco-Roman harbor at Matala in the west (*AR* 1971-2, 23).

NIPIDITOS PEDIADOS: In 1956, Platon dug a large shaft grave which had been robbed; a building nearby appeared to belong to the LM I period (*KCh* 1956, 417).

NIROU KHANI: In 1918–19 Xanthoudides excavated at Nirou Khani, about 13 km east of Herakleion, a large LM I building with a store of religious furniture. He also excavated in the LM I port town on the Ayios Theodoros promontory, and located the cemetery site, though all the tombs except one were destroyed by a flood in 1897. Many MM sherds were found in a lower level (*AD* 1918, 136ff) (*AE* 1922, 1ff) (cf. Evans, *P. of M.* 2, 279ff).

In 1916 and 1929–30, Marinatos excavated in the Ayios Theodoros settlement. Many of the remains are submerged; cuttings in the rock indicate the existence of a Minoan dockyard (*PAE* 1925–6, 141ff). Platon reported that during work at the 'Shrine of the Double Axes' a pit containing hundreds of conical cups and remains of sacrifices was found beneath the threshold of a doorway (*AR* 1945–7, 118).

PANAGIA MONOFATSIOU: At 'Patela' near here fragments of early MM clay figurines were found, possibly indicating a peak sanctuary, and a Greek statuette of a seated goddess and coins may indicate a later Greek site (*KCh* 1955, 567).

PANAGIA PEDIADOS: On the hill of Kefali, near this village, Halbherr under the auspices of the American Institute of Archaeology, explored a plundered sub-Minoan—proto-Geometric tholos tomb in 1893–94 (*AJA* 1901, 283ff) and the Italian school excavated four more in 1924 (*Ann.* 10-12, 1927–29, 389ff). This was one of the necropoleis of the city on Ayios Ilias hill near Aphrati (q.v.), the site of ancient Arkades.

PETROKEPHALI KAINOURGIOU: At 'Miloi' near this village in the Mesara, the Italian School excavated a proto-Geometric tomb and found a number of vases and iron weapons (*KCh* 11, 1957, 336, 342).

PETROKEPHALO MALEVIZIOU: MM III sherds and burials were noted near this village by Miss Money-Coutts and Miss Eccles in 1934 (*Arch.* 177).

PHAISTOS: Halbherr and Taramelli explored the site of Phaistos for the American Institute of Archaeology in 1894 (*AJA* 5, 1901, 418ff) and with Pernier and the Italian Mission began excavations in 1900. Pernier continued excavations throughout the decade and did restoration and conservation work in the 1930's. In 1949 D. Levi resumed excavations at the site which have continued since. The site, known chiefly for the Minoan palace, was occupied from Neolithic through Hellenistic times, and probably declined with the rise of Gortyn.

Publications include: (Pernier: *Il Palazzo Minoico de Festòs I*, Rome 1935) (Pernier and Banti, *Il Palazzo Minoico de Festòs 2*, Rome 1951) (*Ann.* 35-6, 1957–8, 1ff; 37-8, 1959–60, 431ff; 39-40, 1961–2, 377ff; 569ff; 45-6, 1967–8, 55ff; 47-8, 1969–70, 41ff).

A summary of the excavation was published in 1964 (*Studies in Mediterranean Archaeology*, II, Lund) and some conclusions have been drawn by Levi (*Ann.* 43-4, 1965–6, 313ff).

PHOINIKIA TEMENOUS: A proto-Geometric–Geometric chamber tomb had been excavated near here (Xanthoudides, *AD* 14, 1931-2, 2ff) and in 1967 at 'Drakouliari', Alexiou excavated a small early proto-Geometric chamber tomb containing a pithos cremation; finds included bronze bowls, iron and bronze weapons, and vases (*Ergon* 1967, 124ff).

PLATANOS KAINOURGIOU: At a spot called 'Stavros' about 150 m west of this village in the Mesara, a Minoan cemetery was excavated by Xanthoudides in 1914–15. Three circular tombs with attached antechambers were excavated. A and B are the largest such tombs yet found, having interior diameters of 13.1 and 10.23 m respectively. These tombs were in use probably in EM II–MM II and a large amount of varying material was found. In the antechambers on the east side of tomb A hundreds of small stone vases were found, and many further burials. More than 60 daggers were found in this tomb. Rectangular burial buildings were located on the north side of the site; LM sherds were found in them. Two trenches were found to contain bones and a few cups; they were probably ossuaries for remains cleared out of the tombs to make room for new burials (Xanthoudides, *VTM* 88ff) (Branigan, *Tombs*, passim).

PORTI KAINOURGIOU: In 1906 Xanthoudides excavated at Porti, between the village of Kantila and Vasilika Anogeia, about 4 km northwest of Koumasa, finding MM pithos burials, a rectangular tomb, and a circular tomb of Mesara type. He estimated that the skeletal material from this tomb represented many hundreds of bodies. The inner diameter of the tomb is 6.65 m and material dating from possibly EM I through MM II was found. He also located the settlement to which this cemetery was connected (Xanthoudides, *VTM* 54ff).

PRASAS PEDIADOS: In 1939 and 1940 Platon excavated a house at 'Korakies' near this village above Amnisos. It was built in the late MM period; most sherds are transitional MM III–LM I (*EEKS* 3, 489ff; 4, 271ff) (*AR* 1939–45, 86). Platon continued excavation in 1951. The house was destroyed twice and not rebuilt after the second destruction at the end of LM IA (*PAE* 1951, 246ff).

PRINIAS MALEVIZIOU: The acropolis 'Patela' near this village is probably the site of ancient Rhizenia. Halbherr and John Alden explored the site in 1894 and noted Hellenistic graves, Archaic inscriptions, and building remains (*AJA* 5, 1901, 399ff). Excavations were conducted by the Italian School under Pernier in 1907–8. There are remains of two Archaic temples with which fragments of Archaic sculpture were found. Below the temples was a deposit of the Geometric period. A Hellenistic fortress occupies the west end of the site (final report: *Ann.* 1, 1914, 18ff).

PYRGOS PEDIADOS: In 1918 Xanthoudides excavated a cave or rock shelter at Pyrgos, a headland east of Nirou Khani. Burials were found ranging from sub-Neolithic through EM III larnax burials (*AD* 4, 1918, 136ff). He examined the area again in 1924–25 and found further burials, sherds, and shallow rock cuttings on Pyrgos hill, perhaps the settlement site (*AR* 1924–5, 226).

ROTASI MONOFATSIOU: In 1954 a proto-Geometric tholos tomb was noted at Rotasi, east of Pyrgos, with many vases and two female idols with raised hands, and in 1955 an extensive Geometric cemetery was found between Pyrgos and Rotasi (*KCh* 8, 1954, 516; 9, 1955, 567). In 1957 a hoard of Minoan bronze implements was found at 'Asprolivadha' and nearby the remains of a probable Minoan settlement (*KCh* 1957, 339). In 1958 north of the village Platon excavated an intact Geometric tholos tomb containing about 250 vases, more than 40 burials, and iron weapons (*KCh* 12, 1958, 468) (*BCH* 1959, 734-5).

SAMBA PEDIADOS: At 'Pirgos' near this village, Minoan buildings were noted in 1957 (*KCh* 11, 1957, 339).

SILAMOS: A completely empty chamber tomb of Late Minoan type was found here in 1958 (*BCH* 1959, 740) (*KCh* 12, 1958, 479).

SIVA MALEVIZIOU: An LM III chamber tomb (*KCh* 1, 1947, 633) was excavated near here.

SIVA PYRGIOTISSIS: In 1909 de Sanctis and della Vida in conjunction with the Phaistos excavations dug two EM circular tombs here, south of Phaistos (*Ausonia* 8, 1913, *Suppl.* 13ff).

SKLAVOKAMBOS: In 1930 Marinatos began excavations of a large LM I house at 'Sklavokambos' near Gonies west of Tylissos. Much fine pottery was found. The house was destroyed by fire toward the end of LM I (*BCH* 1930, 516ff) (*AE* 1939–41, 69ff). In 1955 Platon examined LM buildings in the area (*KCh* 1955, 567-8). See also 'Gonies'.

SKOTEINO: Evans explored the large Skoteino Cave, southeast of Gournes, a large vault with broken stalagmites and many galleries, and noted MM sherds (*P. of M.* I, 163). Following some illicit excavations, the cave was re-examined by Davaras in 1963. He recovered votive objects ranging from MM I through Roman, including three LM I bronze statuettes of nude male votaries (*AD* 18, 1963, *Chr.* 2, 312)(Cf. Faure, *Fonctions, 162ff)(KCh* 17, 1963, 398)(Davaras, *BCH* 1969, 620ff).

SMARI PEDIADOS: LM chamber tombs with sarcophagi have been excavated at 'Ston Pitho' in the vicinity of this village north of Kastelli (*KCh* 12, 1958, 479; 13, 1959, 386).

SPILIA: In 1966 Alexiou excavated two rock-cut tombs of an outlying cemetery of the Hellenistic city of Knossos, at a place called 'Serayia' (*AD* 22,1967, *Chr.* 2, 486).

STAMNI PEDIADOS: For LM chamber tombs near this village, see Episkopi.

STAVRAKIA MALEVIZIOU: In 1962 Davaras excavated a Minoan chamber tomb with larnakes (*KCh* 17, 1963, 398).

STRAVOMYTI CAVE: Several times between 1898 and 1924 Evans explored the Stravomyti ('crooked-nose') cave on the southern slopes of Mt. Juktas below the Christos Chapel (*P. of M.* 2, 68ff). Marinatos re-examined the cave in 1949–50 (*PAE* 1949, 108ff; 1950, 248ff). Pottery ranging from Neolithic through Hellenistic or Roman times was found. Apart from an infant skeleton in a Neolithic vase, the cave appears to have been used as a shelter in Neolithic–EM I times. Large 'palace style' storage jars indicate that from MM III to LM I the cave may have served as a store-house. A cult began in LM III times (cf. Faure, *Fonctions,* 173-5).

TEFELI MONOFATSIOU: In 1956, Platon dug an LM III chamber tomb with larnakes. On the height of Parathamna above were traces of a sub-Neolithic building, near where an interesting sub-Neolithic vase was found the year before (*BCH* 81, 1957, 630ff) (*KCh* 1956, 416).

TRYPITI: Alexiou excavated an EM I circular tomb at Trypiti on the south coast in 1967 (*AD* 22, 1967, *Chr.* 2, 484).

TSOUTSOUROS: In 1956, Platon suggested that this village on the coast south of Kastelliana may be the ancient Inatos, where Eiléithyia Inatia was worshipped. In 1962, Platon and Davaras excavated a cave-shrine richly furnished with votives ranging from proto-Geometric to Archaic (Roman votives were also found). The many terracotta figurines illustra-ted the survival of Minoan traditions (*AD* 18, 1963, *Chr.* 2, 310-11) (*AD* 19, 1964, *Chr.* 3, 444).

TYLISSOS: In 1909 a Minoan settlement was found here and Hazzidakis began excavations that continued through 1913. The site consists mainly of three LM I villas, but EM walls and MM material was also found and the site was reoccupied in the LM III period (Hazzidakis, *Les villas minoennes de Tylissos,* École française d'Athènes, *Études Crétoises* 3, Paris 1934). Platon carried out restoration work in 1954–55 and excavated an LM stoa (*AR* 1954, 17; 1955, 30).

In 1962 an MM hill sanctuary at 'Korphi tou Pyrgou' was cleared by Alexiou; male and female figurines, bulls, and cups were found among the ashes of a hearth (*AD* 19, 1964, *Chr.* 440).

TYMBAKI PYRGIOTISSIS: Minoan graves had been reported here (Evans, *P. of M.* 2, 90) (*Mon. Ant.* 9, 1899, 296) and in 1957 three Graeco-

Roman tombs were discovered near the airport; and remains of houses with Kamares sherds were also reported in the area (*AR* 1957, 20) (*KCh* 1957, 339).

VALI: In 1926, Marinatos dug an EM circular tomb near this village, east of Gortyn. It continued in use for quite some time, as MM and LM cups were found in addition to EM III (*AR* 1926–7, 258) (*BCH* 50, 1926, 578).

VASILIKA ANOGEIA KAINOURGIOU: LM III chamber tombs with larnakes have been published by Orsi (*Mon. Ant.* 1890, 1, 203; 14, 1904, 679).

VATHY PEDIADOS: Two LM III larnax burials were excavated in 1903 by Xanthoudides at 'Arta' between Kato Vatheia and Elea (*AE* 1904, 1ff). At 'Kaminia' by Kato Vatheia a proto-Geometric–Geometric chamber tomb was excavated (*AA* 1937, 224).

In 1958 Platon excavated an Archaic pithos burial near Kato Vatheia (*BCH* 1959, 733). Near Ano Vatheia a chamber tomb was excavated in 1964 by Alexiou which contained a decorated larnax and an LM IIIB cup (*AD* 20, 1965, *Chr.* 3, 551-2) (*Ergon* 1964, 131ff).

VATHYPETRO: In 1948 a large Minoan villa of LM I date was discovered here and Marinatos excavated from 1949–56. The building seems to have soon been abandoned, perhaps due to poor construction, and then some of the rooms seem to have been converted into workshops; some of the apparatus is partially preserved. A potter's kiln, wine and olive presses and a loom were found. Brunsig assisted in the excavations (*PAE* 1949, 101ff; 1950, 242ff; 1951, 258ff; 1952, 592ff; 1953, 298; 1955, 309ff; 1965, 223).

In 1956, about 1.5 km away, Platon found a building with pottery and potters' wheels dating to LM I–II times, and in 1957 a building with LM sherds was located south of the main villa (*KCh* 1956, 421; 1957, 339).

VIANNOS: In 1954 and 1956 Platon excavated at Galana Kharakia near Ano Viannos, finding EM III–MM I tombs in the rock with pithos burials.

He also explored a building with four rooms on the height above the tombs. MM I vases were recovered from it. Next to the building is a small circular tomb in which were found two larnakes with bones and EM III–MM I vases (*AR* 1956, 22) (*KCh* 8, 1954, 512; 10, 1956, 416ff) (cf. *BSA* 1964, 83-4. The site had been described by Mariani (*Mon.Ant.* 6, 1895, 332ff) (*RE*, Suppl. 7, 79ff).

VITSILIA PEDIADOS: In 1953, a Neolithic–EM I rock shelter was discovered here (*BCH* 1954, 157) (*AR* 1953, 166).

VONI PEDIADOS: In 1957 Platon investigated this area, finding an LM III bath-shaped sarcophagus, an MM III pithos and a small Minoan settlement site at 'Moulali' and a small bronze double axe at 'Sokhora' (*KCh* 11, 1957, 337) (*AR* 1957, 20).

VOROU: Marinatos excavated two roughly built Minoan circular tombs here in 1931. A large number of small cups in groups of two and three were found, silver earrings, and burials in pithoi and larnakes. Material dates mostly from MM I (*AD* 13, 1930–31, 137ff).

West Central Crete
Nomos Rethymnis

AÏMONAS MYLOPOTAMOU: A large group of Archaic plaques and figurines were found here in 1963, most of the figurines representing a naked goddess (*KCh* 17, 1963, 412) (*AD* 19, 1964, *Chr.* 3, 447).

AMARI: Some sites in the Amari valley are grouped together under one village. See Apodoulou, Apostoloi, Ellenes, Meronas, Monasteraki, Patsos, Thronos (Sybrita), Vizari.

APODOULOU AMARIOU: After Pendlebury saw an inscribed steatite vase in 1933 (*Arch.*, 175), Marinatos excavated on the 'Gournes' hill about l km northwest of the village, and uncovered a settlement and large villa built during MM III and destroyed at the end of LM I (*AA* 1933, 297; 1935, 246ff) (*AD* 15, 1933–5, par. 54-5). Jantzen excavated further house remains in 1942 and found another inscribed stone vase (Matz, *Forschungen auf Kreta*, 137ff). Some of the finds from the site suggest the presence of a shrine. Pendlebury reported seeing EM sherds (*Arch.* 289) but the finds from the excavations are all MM III–LM I.

In 1961 Davaras excavated an LM III tholos tomb at 'Sopatakia' above the road from Rethymnon. The report of this excavation (*AD* 18, 1963, *Chr.* 2, 315) states that the tomb is located above the road *west* of the village and that the megaron excavated by Marinatos lay 500 meters to the south. Actually the road curves to the northwest (as corrected by Davaras), and the Megaron is 1000 meters to the west. In 1962 Hood and Warren located the tholos 300 meters north of the village, and about l km east of the megaron site (*BSA* 1964, 78; map of area, 79). They also noted traces of MM or later occupation on the 'Khalepa' hill north of the tholos.

Further to the south of Apodoulou other sites have been noted. At Mandres, near the junction of the road from Apodoulou with the road from Tymbaki there are remains of a Roman house and LM III larnakes have been reported (*KCh* 12, 1958, 481). North of this at 'Kastri' toward Vromonero, a Graeco-Roman city site was noted (Pashley, *Travels* 2, 303-4) (*BSA* 42, 1947, 188). It is possibly the site of ancient Psykhion. South of Kastri Graeco-Roman remains, possibly a sanctuary, were noted in 1962 (*BSA* 1964, 78ff).

APOSTOLOI AMARIOU: Platon described a Minoan settlement near Apostoloi and LM III tombs dug by Petroulakis near Yena village (*KCh* 1, 1947, 638) but these could not be traced in 1962 (*BSA* 1964, 72).

ARGYROUPOLIS: Argyroupolis is the site of ancient Lappa. The remains have been described by Pashley (*Travels* 1, 83-4), Spratt (*Travels* 2, 117ff), and Thenon (*RA* n.s. 15, 1867, 265ff). Pendlebury noted Classical walls in 1935 (*Arch.* 350) and Hellenistic tombs on the path from Zouridhi village (*Arch.* 360). A Classical statuette of a woman holding an apple was found in 1963.

In 1969 part of a Roman building, perhaps a bath complex, was excavated. A life-size statue of Aphrodite of the first century AD was found (*AD* 25, 1970, *Chr.* 2, 476).

ARMENOI: In 1969 and 1970, I. Tzedakis excavated more than twenty chamber tombs in an LM IIIA–B cemetery. The tombs are of an unusual type, in that most of them have a dromos. A number of painted larnakes with scenes probably of religious ceremonies were recovered, along with other larnakes, pottery, jewelry and seals (*AAA* 4, 1971, 216ff) (*AD* 25, 1970, *Chr.* 2, 476-7).

ATSIPADA AY. VASILIOU: At a place called 'Pezoulo', E. Petroulakis excavated twenty-one LM III–sub-Minoan pithos burials in 1912–13, finding vases and figurines (*AE* 1915, 48ff).

At 'Fonises' and 'Lakkos' east of the village, traces of an extensive LM III refuge settlement were noted in 1965 by Hood and Warren (*BSA* 1966, 178-9).

AXOS MYLOPOTAMOU: Axos appears to have been first settled at the end of the Late Minoan era, and to have become fully established by the eighth century. Most of the important archaeological finds are of the Archaic period. In 1899 the Italian School under Halbherr excavated part of the site, including a large megaron-shaped building, possibly an Archaic temple of Aphrodite, and another temple in the lower city. A number of inscriptions were also found, including a late Archaic law code. Only brief descriptions of these excavations were published at the time (*Rendiconti dell' Acc. Lincei* 5, 1899, 37-9; 6, 1900, 311-12). Taramelli described some of the finds (*Mon. Ant.* 9, 1899, 308ff). Levi published a fuller description of the excavation and of the bronze finds much later, from Halbherr's notebooks, shortly after Halbherr's death (*Ann.* 13-14, 1930–1, 43ff).

In 1914 Petroulakis excavated briefly, recovering votives of the 4th century BC from a Demeter temple (*AE* 1915). Two further fragments of an Archaic law code were found by Hutchinson and Miss Jeffrey (*AR* 1945–7, 118). In 1961 Alexiou found a life-size Archaic head and an Archaic poros Gorgoneion (*AD* 17, 1961–2, *Chr.* 300) (Davaros, 'Dadalische Statue aus Astritsi', *Antike Kunst*, Beiheft 8, 1972).

AYIA GALINI AYIOU VASILIOU: Ayia Galini is probably the site of ancient Soulia. Ancient remains, including a sanctuary of Artemis, have been described by Halbherr (*AJA* 11, 1896, 593ff) and De Sanctis (*Mon. Ant.* 9, 1899, 535ff). Hood and Warren noted a site, perhaps the city itself, on a hill northeast of the village in 1961 (*BSA* 1966, 167).

An ancient wreck in the waters between Ayia Galini and Kokkinos Pyrgos was explored in 1937 by Theophanes. Hellenistic and Roman bronzes, coins, and some copper ingots were recovered (*EEKS* 1, 1938, 610ff) (*AA* 1937, 229ff). Leatham and Hood visited it in 1955, but at the time it was largely covered with sand (*BSA* 1958–9, 280). In 1960 Platon and Davaras examined it, and recovered more bronzes and over 250 coins, mostly of the 3rd century AD (*AD* 16, 1960, 257).

AYIOS VASILIOS PROVINCE: Sinclair Hood and Peter Warren surveyed part of Ayios Vasilios Province in 1961. Surface indications of many sites of all periods were noted. The most important are listed separately. Reference should be made to their report (*BSA* 61, 1966, 163ff) for other sites.

ELEUTHERNA MYLOPOTAMOU: The site of Eleutherna, including houses and temples, Classical walls, Roman cisterns, and a Classical bridge in the valley to the northwest, had been described by Spratt (*Travels* 2, 89ff) and Mariani (*Mon. Ant.* 6, 1896, 193ff). Also, a Daedalic statue was found here (*RA* 1893, 10ff).

In 1929, the British School under Payne, with Hogarth and Miss Hartley, excavated on the slopes of the acropolis, finding mostly Hellenistic and Roman material. On the western side of the acropolis, at 'Orthe Petra', a large deposit of Geometric pottery was uncovered, along with some sub-Minoan and proto-Geometric. There were also fragments of a mid-sixth century Laconian crater. Terrace walls in this area were dated to the Classical period (*BSA* 30, 1928–30, 266ff; 31, 1930–31, 108ff).

In 1956 Alexiou recovered parts of two first century AD statues from the north of the acropolis (*KCh* 10, 1956, 421-2) and in 1960, he found fragments of Archaic inscriptions.

ELLENES AMARIOU: After three LM bronze axes, a larnax, and a pithos were found in 1930 at the foot of the Petri hill northwest of the village and to the west of the road, Marinatos excavated here in 1931–32. He reported EM houses on the summit with 'Pyrgos' style pottery and a late Minoan settlement on the slopes of the hill. He also reported Neolithic celts. He also visited the Maryiles cave east of the village and reported Neolithic, EM and abundant MM sherds (*AJA* 36, 1932, 60-1) (*AA* 1932, 177; 1933, 295ff). Faure reported obsidian and sherds of all Minoan periods and Geometric periods in front of the cave (*BCH* 1956, 98). In 1962 Hood and Warren visited the area and found the site on the Petri hill much eroded. They found an obsidian blade, and sherds of MM I or II at the latest (*BSA* 1964, 73-4).

GOULEDIANA RETHYMNOU: In 1935 Pendlebury visited a site called 'Ornithe' or 'Orinthe' and noted Archaic and later walls and sherds (*Arch.* 340, 350, 360, 370). He suggested this as the site of ancient Osmida. Platon examined the site in 1952 and found substantial traces of the ancient city. In 1954–56 he excavated houses of the 8th–7th century, finding fragments of bronze vases, relief pithoi and vases. He suggested this as the site of ancient Phalanne (*KCh* 8, 1954, 510; 9, 1955, 556-7; 10, 1956, 410-11) (*PAE* 1954, 377ff; 1955, 298ff; 1956, 229ff) (*AA* 1940, 305).

IDAIAN CAVE: This important cave, which had been known locally as the 'Voskopoulos Cave', was explored by Halbherr and Greek archaeologists in 1885, after shepherds had found antiquities in it. Outside the cave were found an altar, iron implements and armor, bone objects, images of animals, bronze tripods and cauldrons, a tympanon, and the famous bronze shields with relief designs. Sherds and other material were found within the cave (*Museo Ital. di ant. class.*, 1888, 689ff). Most of this material dates from the eighth century BC and later, though the dating particularly of the bronze shields, is controversial (on the dating of the shields: A. Frothingham, *AJA* 1888, 431ff; E. Kunze, *Kretische Bronzereliefs*, Stuttgart, 1931; S. Benton, *BSA* 39, 1938–9, 52ff).

In 1917 Xanthoudides conducted a short excavation (*AD* 1918, *Par.* 23). In 1956 Marinatos began further exploration of the cave and found some LM III ceramics, a large amount of other pottery, fragments of bronze shields and tripods, gold leaves, and Egyptian faience. He also located an internal wall in the cave and evidence of sacrificial fires. Also in 1956 he excavated a building below the cave in the Nidha plain and found fragments of late Roman vases dedicated to Zeus (*Ergon* 1956, 108ff) (cf. *BCH* 1956, 97-8; 1957, 632). (For the identification of the cave with the Idaean cave of Zeus: Fabricius, *AM* 1885, 59ff; 280ff). Faure gives a summary of material and evidence for the cult of Zeus, the Curetes, and initiation rituals (*Fonctions*, 99ff).

KERAME AYIOU VASILIOU: Traces of walls and sherds on the site of an ancient city south of the town at 'Pirgos' and 'Kionia' have been noted by Pendlebury (*Arch.* 293,340), Kirsten (Matz, *Forschungen auf Kreta* 125) and Hood and Warren (*BSA* 1966, 173-4).

KHOUMERI MYLOPOTAMOU: At 'Laria' at Khoumeri near Perama two LM III chamber tombs with larnax and pithos burials were excavated by Platon in 1951 (*KCh* 1951, 445; 1952, 479). Roman tombs and traces of a small Roman settlement were noted in 1962 (*BSA* 1964, 55).

KOUMI RETHYMNOU: A probable LM III chamber tomb is reported from Koumi (*KCh* 2, 1948, 589).

MAROULAS RETHYMNOU: Three LM III chamber tombs with larnax burials were excavated in 1963 (*KCh* 17, 1963, 412) (*AD* 19, 1964, *Chr.* 3, 447). The larnax was published by Kanta.

MELAMBES AYIOU VASILIOU: Platon identified a site here as ancient Korion after recovering two inscriptions in 1959 (*KCh* 13, 1959, 391) (cf. *BSA* 1966, 169-70).

MELIDHONI MYLOPOTAMOU: On the south side of the ridge to the northwest of the village is the cave 'Yerospilios' which was dedicated to Hermes in Classical times. The cave has been only slightly excavated. It was described by Pashley (*Travels* 2, 126ff), and Geometric to Hellenistic and Roman material noted (cf. Pendlebury, *Arch.* 346, 350). In 1956 an LM I bronze double axe was reported from the cave (*KCh* 1956, 421) and in 1961 Alexiou reported LM IIIB vases (*KCh* 17, 1963, 393). Neolithic material has also been found in the cave (cf. Faure, *Fonctions,* 131ff).

In 1962 an EM–MM settlement site was noted on the hill at the west end of the ridge (*BSA* 1964, 58-9).

MESI RETHYMNOU: LM III tombs with larnax burials were discovered by peasants in 1891(*BCH* 1892, 295ff) and a Late Minoan tholos tomb in 1963 (*KCh* 17, 1963, 412) (*AD* 19, 1964, *Chr.* 3, 447).

MIXORROUMA AY. VASILIOU: In 1960, Alexiou noted an LM building where a stone lamp had previously been found near this village west of Spilion (*AR* 1960, 25).

MONASTERAKI AMARIOU: At 'Kharakas' north of the village, a Minoan town was noted by Pendlebury (*Arch.* 291) and excavated by Kirsten and Grundmann in 1942 (Matz, *Forschungen auf Kreta,* 27ff). Stretches of Cyclopean walls in places 2 meters high, houses, and traces of what was perhaps a small palace on the summit, were found. The site was occupied mostly during MM, probably until the end of LM I.

Northwest of this site, at 'Ayia Kyriaki', an LM site which had been excavated by the local schoolmaster was noted by Pendlebury (*Arch.* 293). (cf. *BSA* 1964, 75-6).

PANGALOKHORI RETHYMNOU: North of the Arsani Monastery

north of this village the road cuts through the remains of an LM III chamber tomb. A larnax and 3 vases were found in it in 1940 (*EEKS* 4, 1941, 268-9).

PANORMOS MYLOPOTAMOS: Panormos was important in the Roman period; remains are mostly Christian and Medieval. Spratt described considerable remains at 'Roumeli Kastelli' (*Travels* 2, 113).

PATSOS AMARIOU: The cave of Ayios Antonios north of Patsos was dedicated to Hermes Kranaios in antiquity. Peasants removed antiquities from the cave in 1885, but there was no systematic excavation. The material found ranges from LM III through Geometric, Hellenistic and Roman (*AJA* 1896, 593). Faure visited the cave in 1961 and recovered LM III votive statuettes, of human and animal figures (*Fonctions*, 136ff).

Further north Alexiou recovered LM I sherds from the 'Fournari' cave in the gorge in 1960 (*AR* 1960, 25). (On caves in the gorge in general cf. *BSA* 1966, 185ff) (*BCH* 1965, 53ff; 1969). Davaras has catalogued and discussed bronze statuettes of worshippers from various sites including Patsos (*BCH* 1969, 620ff).

PERAMA MYLOPOTAMOU: In 1935 Pendlebury noted a site on the 'Grivila' hill about 1.5 km northeast of Perama and about 1 km west of the cave of Hermes at Melidhoni (*Arch.* 262, 370). A bronze stauette of a worshipper was found in 1951 and Platon conducted a trial excavation, finding abundant LM I sherds and traces of proto-Geometric–Geometric houses (*KCh* 1951, 441) (*BCH* 1953, 240). In 1962 a stone axe, Neolithic sherds and numerous LM III sherds were found (*BSA* 1964, 56-8).

PIGI RETHYMNOU: An LM III chamber tomb was excavated at 'Skoundi' (*AA* 1940, 305), and in 1968 a chamber tomb was excavated at 'Grambela' which contained eight sarcophagi and forty-two vases of the LM IIIA–B period (*AD* 24, 1969, *Chr.* 2, 435).

PREVELI AYIOU VASILIOU: At 'Elliniko' near Kato Preveli a Roman bath or villa and cist graves were noted by Platon (*KCh* 1, 1947, 638) and Kirsten (Matz, *Forschungen auf Kreta*, 126). At the mouth of the Megas Potamos, Kirsten noted a Roman settlement in 1942 (ibid.) (cf. *BSA* 1966, 180-2).

RETHYMNON: An LM III chamber tomb was found in 1947 in the Mastaba suburb southeast of the town center (*KCh* 1, 1947, 638ff). Another group of tombs was located about 100 m to the west (*BSA* 1964, 60). There is a basic bibliography (Kalokyris, *Archaia Rithymna* 1950).

There is a very important peak sanctuary at Vrysinas excavated in 1972–74 by Davaras (*AAA* 7, 1974, 210ff).

SAKTOURIA AYIOU VASILIOU: Minoan remains have been noted in the area south of Saktouria toward the coast and MM II/III–LM I sherds were noted. A Minoan idol was found in 1947 and is now in the Rethymnon Museum (*AD* 17, 1961–2, *Chr.* 300) (cf. *BSA* 1966, 171-72).

SISE MYLOPOTAMOU: At Sise Alexiou reports the discovery in 1965 of an inscribed block of Hellenistic date which indicated the existence of a city of the 'Sisaians' (*AD* 21, 1966 *Chr.* 2, 407ff).

STAVROMENOS RETHYMNOU: Ancient Agrion may have been near here. Xanthoudides described traces of a Graeco-Roman town at 'Palaio-kastro' east of the village (*AD* 4, 1918, *Par.* 14-15) (*AD* 6, 1920–1, *Par.* 163-4). There was also a Minoan settlement here; MM–LM I and LM III sherds were noted in 1962 (*BSA* 1964, 62). Alexiou excavated an LM III chamber tomb with five painted larnakes in 1960 (*AD* 16, 1960, 272) (*Ergon*, 1960, 212). Roman graves were also noted (*BCH* 1960, 202ff). Other Minoan and Classical sites are known in the area of Khamalevri (*BSA* 1964, 62ff).

THRONOS AMARIOU: The ancient city of Sybrita, most important in the Roman period, included the area of the village of Thronos. The center of the city was the Kefala hill northwest of the village. The site was partially excavated by Kirsten in 1942 (Matz, *Forschungen auf Kreta*, 142ff). There was also an extensive LM III settlement on the summit. In 1954 a series of poros slabs with carved triglyphs, six of them bearing proxeny decrees, came to light in roadmaking south of the village (*KCh* 8, 1954, 517) (cf. *BSA* 1964, 71-2).

VIRAN EPISKOPI MYLOPOTAMOU: In 1959 Kalokyris, while excavating an important early Christian church, found traces of a Hellenistic shrine which he suggests was a sanctuary of Artemis Diktynna (*KCh* 1959, 379) (*BCH* 1960, 849-50).

VIZARI AMARIOU: West of the village are the remains of a town of the Roman period, of which an Early Christian basilica has been excavated by K. Kalokyris (*PAE* 1956, 250ff) (*Ergon* 1958, 177ff).

YERANI RETHYMNOU: I. Tzedakis excavated a previously unknown cave at 'Kyani Akti'. It was in use throughout the Neolithic period. Pottery, figurines, and obsidian and bone tools were found, and skeletons of humans and animals including deer. The cave entrance had been blocked by falling rock at the end of the Neolithic period (*AD* 25, 1970, *Chr.* 2, 474ff).

Western Crete
Nomos Khanion

AKROTIRI PENINSULA: Numerous sites, particularly caves, have been noted on the Akrotiri Peninsula. For a survey of sites on the peninsula see Paul Faure (*BCH* 1960, 211ff) and for caves in the vicinity of the Gouverneto Monastery, the article by U. Jantzen (F. Matz, *Forschungen auf Kreta*, 1ff).

The Cave of Lera, near Stavros in the northwest of the peninsula was first explored by Paul Faure in 1959 (*BCH* 1960, 213-14; 1962, 46-47) (*KCh* 1961–2, 195ff) (Faure, *Fonctions*, 140ff). The cave was thoroughly excavated by Davaras in 1966. Finds included sherds of all periods from Neolithic to Byzantine, Classical and Hellenistic lamps, figurines and reliefs. The cult in the cave appears to have begun in LM III and inscriptions on some of the Classical sherds indicate that Pan and the Nymphs were worshipped (*AD* 22, 1967, *Chr.* 2, 496ff).

Several caves were investigated by Jantzen in 1942: In the 'Koumaro' Cave were found Neolithic burials and vases, some MM sherds and LM III stirrup jars (Jantzen, op.cit., 1ff). Jantzen reported material from LM through Classical on the terrace in front of the 'Arkouda' or 'Panayia' cave (ibid., 4-5) and Faure reported material perhaps going back to the Geometric period, but mostly Classical and Hellenistic, from the cave (*BCH* 1960, 211-12) (Faure, *Fonctions*, 144ff). Alexiou reported 5th century clay plaques of Artemis and Apollo from the cave (*AR* 1960, 25).

A Late Minoan settlement and cemetery has been noted near the Ayia Triada Monastery by Faure (*BCH* 1959, 749; 1960, 212-3) and Alexiou (*AD* 17, 1961–2, *Chr.* 300) in 1960–61.

The site of ancient Minoa had been noted by Spratt (*Travels* 1, 130) and walls and houses of Roman date were excavated by B. Theophanides in 1939 (*EEKS* 3, 481ff).

APTERA: From the fifth century BC onwards this city on the south side of

Suda Bay was one of the chief commercial cities of Crete. The extensive remains have been described by Pashley, who visited the site in 1834 (*Travels* 2, 36ff), and inscriptions were published by Haussolier (*BCH* 1879, 418). Mariani visited and described the site in 1893 (*Mon. Ant.* 6, 1895, 208ff). The site was visited and planned by H. Drerup in 1942 (Matz, *Forschungen auf Kreta*, 87ff). Remains of defense walls, temples, a theatre, and Roman cisterns can be seen.

Alexiou investigated the site in 1957–58 and excavated a small Roman temple. He explored the rest of the site, and removed inscriptions and fragments of sculpture to the Khania Museum (*KCh* 12, 1958, 468-9) (*BCH* 1959, 749ff).

ASPROSIKIA APOKORONOU: Theophanides noted LM III and later sherds in the 'Korakia' cave in 1937 (*AE* 1948–9, *Chr.* 11-12). Faure noted MM I, MM III and Roman sherds, and human bones at the cave entrance (*BCH* 1956, 98).

AYIA MARINA KYDONIAS: The Yerospilia cave near the village was explored by Marinatos ('Höhlenforschungen in Kreta', 1928, 6ff) and Faure (*BCH* 1958, 501). It was apparently a late EM and early MM burial cave.

AYIA ROUMELI SPHAKION: In 1959 G. and S. Weinberg conducted a trial excavation at the site of ancient Tarrha on the coast near Ayia Roumeli in the hope of locating a glass factory believed to exist here. They confirmed that Tarrha was occupied from the 5th century BC until the 5th century AD. They found a large quantity of glass fragments; they opened 5th–4th century BC tombs, Roman tombs, and studied the Roman remains (*Hesperia* 29, 1960, 90ff).

DEBLA: Debla is a summit in the foothills of the White Mountains southwest of Khania, 542 m high. In 1971 P. Warren and I. Tzedakis investigated an EM settlement, uncovering plans of three buildings and traces of a fourth. It was occupied during EM I–II. The site is one of the few excavated EM I open settlement sites in Crete (*AAA* 5, 1972, 66ff).

DIKTYNNA: The site of the Greek and Roman temple of Artemis Diktynna on Cape Spathi had long been used as a quarry for stones. R. Pococke described the remains (*Description of the East and some other Countries* 2.1, 244-45) and Spratt later visited the site (*Travels* 2, 197).

The temple was excavated by the Germans in 1942. The site appears to go back to the 9th century BC. The temple was rebuilt several times, lastly under Hadrian in the second century AD (G. Welter and U. Jantzen in Matz, *Forschungen auf Kreta*, 106ff).

DRAMIA APOKORONOU: Dramia is the site of ancient Hydramon or Hydramia, which reached its peak in Roman times. LM III tombs have been discovered in the area (*KCh* 5, 1951, 445; 6, 1952, 479ff). In 1955 a marble head, probably of Artemis, was discovered at 'Vardia' (*KCh* 9, 1955, 568).

HYRTAKINA: The site of ancient Hyrtakina is at 'Kastro' near Temenia Selinou. Remains, from the Archaic to Roman periods, have been described by Pashley (*Travels* 2, 3) and Savignoni (*Mon. Ant.* 11, 1901, 408). Theophanides excavated a temple in 1939 (*EEKS* 2, 1939, 528; 3, 1940, 485).

KALAMI APOKORONOU: I. Tzedakis excavated five LM IIIA–B chamber tombs along the National Highway. Fine pottery, bronze tools, and weapons were found. One pyxis is decorated with birds, double axes, and a man playing a cithara (*AAA* 2, 1969, 365ff; 3, 1970, 111-2) (*AD* 25, 1970, *Chr.* 2, 468-9).

KANTANOS SELINOU: This is probably the site of ancient Kantanos, though the exact location is disputed. Theophanides excavated a large Roman building 30 m on a side, and a statue base with an inscription of Septimius Severus. The building was perhaps the Roman praetorium in the vicinity (*EEKS* 1, 1938, 606ff).

KASTELLI KISAMOU: The town occupies the site of ancient Kissamos, a port of Polyrrhenia. Ancient remains in the vicinity were noted by many, including Pococke in 1745 (*Descriptions*, 2, 245), Pashley (*Travels* 2, 43), and Savignoni (*Mon. Ant.* 11, 1901, 304).

The ancient acropolis, located at a place called Seli, west of the town, was excavated by Theophanides (*EEKS* 1, 604). The ancient port was located at Mavro Molo. The area was explored in 1966. Finds included a Hellenistic or Roman statue of a satyr, a large Roman building which is probably a bath complex, a cistern, and part of an aquaduct. Excavations continued through 1969. A large house with some mosaic floors was cleared. The earliest building phase of the house was the second half of the 3rd century AD (*AD* 22, 1967, *Chr.* 2, 498ff; *AD* 23, 1968, *Chr.* 2, 416-7; *AD* 24, 1969, *Chr.* 2, 431-2; *AD* 25, 1970, *Chr.* 2, 471ff).

KAVOUSI KISAMOU: At Kavousi near Platanos in the northwest, a chamber tomb with proto-Geometric and Geometric vases was found in 1969 (*KCh* 1969, 542) (*AR* 1970–71, 32).

KHANIA: Numerous Bronze Age tombs have been reported in and around Khania; LM III chamber tombs are numerous, particularly in the Mazali area above the Law Courts. Mariani reported tombs in 1895 (*Mon. Ant.* 6, 1895, 201ff). Further tombs were reported (*AM* 25, 1900, 466) (*AD* 6, 1920, *Par.* 164-65) and in 1938 Theophanides began excavating, finding LM III tombs in the Mazali area, MM I tombs between Khalepa and Profitis Elias on the east side of the town, MM III tombs near the eastern corner of the Venetian fortress, Hellenistic tombs east of the modern cemetery of Ayios Loukas on the south side of town, and a late Hellenistic mosaic depicting Poseidon and a nymph from Nea Katastimata (*EEKS* 1, 1938, 609; 2, 1939, 528ff; 3, 1940, 484; 4, 1941, 268) (*AE* 1948–9, 12ff: 1938 excavations). The Germans excavated further graves in 1942 and these are reported, along with a list of previously known LM III chamber tombs, by U. Jantzen (Matz, *Forschungen auf Kreta,* 72ff).

Since the war, more Minoan graves have been found in the Mazali area (*KCh* 6, 1952, 480; 7, 1953, 490-1), and Platon and Davaras excavated the entire LM III cemetery in 1958–61 (*KCh* 12, 1958, 482; 13, 1959, 376; 14, 1960, 515; 17, 1963, 392) (*AD* 16, 1960, 272; *AD* 17, 1961–2, 291-2). In 1966, seven Classical tombs were excavated in the Mazali area, and it appears that the Classical and Roman necropolis as well as the LM III cemetery was located here (*AD* 22, 1967, *Chr.* 2, 497-8).

At Ayia Kiriaki in the Khalepa suburb on the east of the town Platon excavated four LM IIIB chamber tombs (*AD* 17, 1961–2, 292-3).

In 1964 I. Tzedakis began a series of important excavations within the Kastelli, which since 1969 have continued as a joint Greek-Swedish excavation under Tzedakis and C.-G. Styrenius. Material of all periods from Neolithic through Graeco-Roman was found. Work was concentrated on the important Minoan levels. The importance of this site has led to a firmer identification of Khania as the ancient Kydonia (*AD* 20, 1965, *Chr.* 3, 568-9; *AD* 21, 1966, *Chr.* 2, 425ff; *AD* 22, 1967, *Chr.* 2, 500ff; *AD* 23, 1968, *Chr.* 2, 413ff; *AD* 24, 1969, *Chr.* 2, 423ff; *AD* 25, 1970, *Chr.* 2, 465ff) (*AAA* 3, 1970, 100ff; 5, 1972, 387ff; 6, 1973, 439ff). Numerous fragments of inscribed tablets and seal impressions have been found, many in Linear A script (Tzedakis, *Kadmos* 6, 1967, 106ff) (Hallager, *AAA* 5, 1972, 508ff; J. Papapostolou, *AAA* 6, 1973, 430ff).

A Roman bath building with mosaics was discovered in a rescue excavation in 1967 (*AD* 25, 1970, *Chr.* 2, 467-8). Faure explored a Neolithic dwelling cave in the Ayios Ioannis district (*BCH* 1962, 45).

KOLYMBARI KISAMOU: On the 'Riza' hill above 'Ayia Irini' near Grimbiliani, southwest of Kolymbari, Alexiou noted an important LM III or earlier settlement (*AD* 16, 1960, *Chr.* 271). Archaic, Classical and Hellenistic sherds were noted by Faure (*BCH* 1962, 54) and he suggests this is the site of ancient Polichna. It is probably the site which Spratt (*Travels* 2, 106) identified as Pergamon (cf. *BSA* 1965, 105). See also Nokhia.

LISSOS: In 1957 Platon explored the site of the sanctuary of Asclepios at Lissos, the Modern Aï Kirkos Selinou on the south coast east of Souia. He noted a small Doric temple, twenty statues and statuettes, as well as what may be the position of the original spring serving the sanctuary. In 1958 he excavated the temple, recovering votive statues and statuettes and their inscribed bases (*KCh* 11, 1957, 336-7) (*BCH* 1958, 798-9; 1959, 753-4).

MALEME KYDONIAS: In 1966 Davaras excavated a tholos tomb with a rectangular chamber. The tomb had long been known, and had been pillaged, but LM III sherds and two cylinder seals were found (*Ergon* 1966, 144ff). There is a basic bibliography (*PAE* 1966, 185ff).

The site was explored by H. Prinz (*AM* 35, 1910, 150). The tomb was damaged by a bomb during the war. The site was visited by Faure (*BCH* 1958, 498) and Hood (*BSA* 60, 1965, 106).

MELIDHONI APOKORONOU: Faure noted several caves in this vicinity, of Neolithic, Minoan and later use (*BCH* 1962, 42-43) (*Fonctions*, 61 passim), and a Minoan vase with an octopus design was found in a small cave near the village (*KCh* 17, 1963, 393).

MESKLA KYDONIAS: This village is the center of an ancient city whose name is not known. Remains of possibly Archaic walls, fragments of a temple, indications of other sanctuaries, and early Christian remains have been found.

Margherita Guarducci suggested that this was ancient Polichna (*Riv. di Filologia* 1936, 153ff); Paul Faure thought that it was the city of the Keraïtes (*BCH* 1962, 49ff).

MODI KYDONIAS: In 1953, Platon excavated a group of seven proto-Geometric tombs with vases, iron weapons, instruments and ornaments (*KCh* 7, 1953, 485) (*BCH* 77, 1953, 240).

NOKHIA KISAMOU: Pendlebury noted Graeco-Roman sherds in the area of Nokhia (*Arch.*, 270, 360), and E. Kirsten described what he identified as Graeco-Roman remains on the Siopata (or Isopata) Hill outside the town. He identified the site as ancient Pergamon, believing that this was the site identified as Pergamon by Spratt (Spratt's site was probably at Ayia Irini near Grimbiliani. See Kolymbari). Faure also noted Archaic-Roman pottery here (*BCH* 1958, 497), and at a later visit identified pottery as late LM, also probably MM III–LM I (*BCH* 1962, 54-5). In 1960 Hood, however, found only apparently Minoan sherds, and he identified the remains on the hill as an extensive settlement ranging from MM III or earlier to LM III (*BSA* 60, 1965, 105).

Pendlebury noted MM sherds by the church of Ayios Konstantinos north of the village (*Arch.* 291) and Hood noted some apparently Minoan sherds in 1960. He also found a Minoan pithos burial further to the north at 'Kambos' (*BSA* 60, 1965, 105).

PERIVOLIA KYDONIAS: Tzedakis excavated in the Mameloukou Trypa cave outside the village in 1968 and 1969. The cave was used as a sanctuary; offering vases indicate that the cave was in use from late MM II to late MM III or LM I. The cave was later reoccupied in the LM IIIB period (*AD*

24, 1969, *Chr.* 2, 434; *AD* 25, 1970, *Chr.* 2, 469ff) (*Ergon* 1968, 102ff) (*PAE* 1968, 133ff).

PHALASARNA: This site on the west coast of Crete was noted by Pashley (*Travels* 2, 62ff) and Spratt (*Travels* 2, 226ff). It was an important Classical and Hellenistic town, and possibly served as a port for Polyrrhenia. Its harbor installations are now inland due to the possible tilting of Crete or local changes. In 1960, Alexiou noted 4th century BC graves, Classical walls, and remains of probable temples (*BCH* 1961, 896). In 1968 a cemetery was discovered, and good pottery recovered. The discovery of an Archaic Corinthian aryballos indicated earlier settlement than had been previously suspected (*AD* 24, 1969, *Chr.* 2, 431ff).

PLATYVOLA CAVE: In the early 1960's villagers found Neolithic and EM II sherds in this cave about 25 km from Khania, near the village of Skourakhlada Kydonias (*AD* 20, 1965, *Chr.* 3, 569-70). The cave was excavated from 1965–67 by Tzedakis. Finds were of considerable interest. Late Neolithic and sub-Neolithic periods were richly represented. Sherds of mature pre-Palatial vases and three pieces of EM sauce boats were found. The collection of Neolithic incised ware was the richest found in any cave in Crete. Vases of 'Vasiliki' ware were common, and 'Pyrgos' ware appeared. Some of the vases resembled those found in Kythera. Outside the cave, Geometric and Classical sherds were found. Several other caves were located in the area, with finds varying from Minoan to Roman times (*AD* 21, 1966, *Chr.* 2, 428-9; *AD* 22, *Chr.* 2, 504ff; *AD* 23, *Chr.* 2, 415ff) (*KCh* 18, 1964, 291; 19, 1965, 297ff).

POLYRRHENIA: Located south of Kastelli Kisamou, this was a large city in Archaic, Classical and Roman times; walls, the remains of public buildings and an aqueduct are visible. Halbherr, in a short excavation, exposed part of a Hellenistic wall, and Savignoni and De Sanctis explored the site in 1899 and described the remains (*Mon. Ant.* 11, 1901, 314ff). In 1938 Theophanides excavated more Hellenistic walls (*AE* 1942–4, *Par.* 17ff).

In 1955 Platon reported an interesting grave stele with relief and inscription from a spot called 'Kapodhaki' (*KCh* 9, 1955, 568-9).

POTISTERIA KISAMOU: The Ellinospilios cave at Potisteria has been explored by Marinatos ('Höhlenforschungen in Kreta', 1928, 5ff) and Faure *(BCH* 1956, 99; 1958, 498) (*Fonctions,* passim). Neolithic, LM III and Medieval pottery were found. It was apparently used as a burial cave in the Neolithic period.

RHODOVANI SELINOU: The site of ancient Elyros is near this village. It was described by Pashley (*Travels* 2, 102ff); traces of walls, and aqueduct and theatre are visible. During road-building in the village at 'Xenotaphi' in 1955, four tombs were discovered, one of which contained much jewelry, including a 4th century BC gold earring, and many vases (*KCh* 9, 1955, 569).

SAMONAS APOKORONOU: Two bronze double axes were brought to the Khania museum from this village in 1963. Alexiou noted a Minoan settlement north of the village and conducted trials there (*AD* 19, 1964, *Chr.* 446). It was excavated by Tzedakis in 1965 and dates from post-Palatial times (*AD* 21, 1966, 427-8).

STYLOS APOKORONOU: In 1960 Alexiou noted a site with LM III sherds in the village (*AD* 16, 1960, *Chr.* 271). In 1961 Platon and Davaras excavated an LM III tholos tomb at 'Sternaki' north of the village. It was plundered, but the vault was intact and Hellenistic vases were found placed within the relieving triangle, possibly indicating a cult. Traces of Minoan and Graeco-Roman occupation were found east of the tomb (*AD* 17, 1961-2, 293ff) (*KCh* 17, 1963, 392). In 1970 Davaras re-examined the tomb and excavated the dromos. He located the settlement to which the tomb belonged on the Azogyres hill, and excavated a substantial LM III building (*AAA* 4, 1971, 42ff). There is a basic bibliography (*AE* 1973, 75ff).

TOPOLIA KISAMOU: About 2 km south of this village at 'Ayia Sofia' is a cave where Neolithic, EM I, LM III and later sherds have been noted (Faure, *BCH* 1956, 102) (*BSA* 60, 1965, 104-5).

VRYSES KYDONIAS: At 'Timios Stavros' east of the village, Theophanides excavated two sub-Minoan or proto-Geometric burials (*EEKS* 3, 1940, 485) and Faure reported others (*BCH* 1958, 499ff). At 'Logadhes' northwest of the village center a pithos burial of a child, of the Geometric period, a hoard of bronze objects including two votive double axes, a fibula, and a pin, were excavated (*KCh* 13, 1959, 392) (*AD* 16, 1960, *Chr.* 271) (*BCH* 1961, 895; 1962, 48-9). Northwest of the village Faure explored the Kera Spiliotissa cave, finding Neolithic, EM, LM I–III and Geometric sherds (*BCH* 1958, 500; 1962, 47-8).

References-Periodicals

	The Academy
AA	*Archaeologischer Anzeiger: Beiblatt zum Jahrbuch des Deutschen archäologischen Instituts*
AAA	*Athens Annals of Archaeology*
AD	*Archaiologikon Deltion*
AE	*Archaiologike Ephermeris*
AJA	*American Journal of Archaeology*
AM	*Mitteilungen des deutschen archäologischen Instituts; athenische Abteilung*
Ann.	*Annuario della Scuola Archeologica di Atene*
	Antike Kunst
	Antiquaries Journal
	The Antiquary
	Antiquity
AR	*Archaeological Reports*
	Archaeologia
	Archaeology
	Archaia Rithymna
	Archives des missions scientifiques
	Athenaeum
	Atti del' Istituto Ven. di Scienze, Lettere ed Arti
Ausonia	*Ausonia, Revista della Societa Italiano di Archeologia e Storia dell' Arte*
AZ	*Archäologische Zeitung*
BCH	*Bulletin de Correspondance Hellénique*
Boll. d'Arte	*Bollettino d'Arte del Ministero della pubblica Istruzione*
BSA	*Annual of the British School at Athens*
	Bull. de l'Acad. R. de Danemark
	Classical Review
	Demosieuma tes en Athenais Archaiologikes Etaireias
Deutsche Akademie	*Deutsche Akademie der Wissenschaften* (formerly *königliche Akademie* or *preussische Akademie*) *Abhandlungen, philosophisch-historische Klasse*
EEKS	*Epetiris Etaireias Kritikon Spoudon*
	Eleutheria
Ergon	*To Ergon tes Archaeologikes Etaireias kata to etos. . .*
	Ethnos
	Gnomon
Hesperia	*Hesperia, Journal of the American School of Classical Studies at Athens*
	Historia
ILN	*Illustrated London News*
JHS	*Journal of Hellenic Studies*
Jahrbuch	*Jahrbuch des deutschen archäologischen Instituts*
Kadmos	*Kadmos: Zeitschrift für vor- und frühgriechische Epigraphik*
	Kathimerini
KCh	*Kretica Chronika*
Memorie	*Memorie dell'Istituto storico-arch. di Rodi*
	Memorie del Reale Istituto Lombardo di Scienze e Lettere
Mon. Ant.	*Monumenti Antichi pubblicati a cura . . . dei Lincei*
	Musée Belge
Museo Italiano	*Museo Italiano di Antichità Classica*
Op. Arch.	*Acta Instituti Romani Regni Sueciae: Opuscula Archaeologica*
Op. Ath.	*Acta Instituti Atheniensis Regni Sueciae: Opuscula Atheniensia*
PAE	*Praktika tes Archaiologikes Etaireias*
	Proc. of the Society of Antiquaries
RA	*Revue Archéologique*

Rendiconti dell'Accademia Lincei
Revue Historique
Rivista di Filologia

Sitzungsb. d.   Sitzungsberichte der Bayerischen Akademie der Wissenschaften, philosophisch-
Bayer. Akad.   philologischen und historischen Classe.

Trans. Am.   Transactions of the American Philosophical Society
Phil. Soc.

Trans. Dept.   Transactions of the Department of Archaeology. Free Museum of Science and
of Arch.   Art, University of Pensylvania

References-Publications

Bent, Aegean   Aegean Islands: The Cyclades or Life Among the Insular Greeks, J.T. Bent. Intro.
Islands   and ed. by A.N. Oikonomedes, Chicago, 1966.

Das ägäische Neolithikum, F. Schachermeyer, Studies in Mediterranean Archaeology, no. 6. Lund, 1964.

Ålin   Das Ende der mykenischen Fundstätten auf dem griechischen Festland, Per Ålin,
Studies in Mediterranean Archaeology. Lund, 1962.

Alt-Ägina, W.W. Wurster. Mainz, 1974.

Alt-Ithaka, Wilhelm Dörpfeld. Munich, 1927.

Ancient Leros, J.L. Benson. Greek, Roman and Byzantine Monographs, no.
3, Durham, N.C. 1963.

Die antike Baureste der Insel Lesbos, R. Koldewey. 1895.

Die Antike Stadt Samos, R. Tölle. Mainz, 1969.

Arch.   The Archaeology of Crete, J.D.S. Pendlebury. London, 1939, reprinted 1967.

Archaeologische Untersuchungen auf Samothrace, A. Conze et al. Vienna,
1875–80.

Archaia Rithymna, Kalokyris. 1950.

Die archaische Kultur der Insel Thera, F. Hiller von Gätringen. Berlin, 1897.

B.M. Cat.   British Museum Catalogue of Greek and Etruscan Vases. London, 1927.

Beiträge zur minoischen Gräberkunde, Ingo Pini. Deutsches Archäologisches
Institut, Weisbaden, 1968.

Branigan,   Tombs of Mesara, K. Branigan. London, 1970.
Tombs

CAH   The Cambridge Ancient History.

The Cemetery at Pachyammos, Crete, R.B. Seager. Univ. of Pennsylvania Museum Anthropological Publications, vol. 7, no. 1, 1916.

CR   Clara Rhodos: studi e materiali pubblicati a cura dell'Istituto storico archaeologico
di Rodi.

CVA   Corpus Vasorum Antiquorum.

Catalogue Musèe d'Histoire. Neuchatel, Switzerland.

Catalogue of the Herakleion Museum, J. Hazzidakis. 1888 (in Greek).

A Companion to Homer, A.J.B. Wace and F.H. Stubbings. 1962.

Corfou, Raymond Matton. Athens, 1960.

The Cretan Collection in Oxford, John Boardman. Oxford, 1961.

Description de l'île de Patmos et de l'île de Samos, Guérin. Paris, 1856.

Description of the East and Some Other Countries, R. Pococke. 1745.

Descriptions . . . des fouilles effectuées à Santorin. H. Gorceix.

Dictionary of Cretan Antiquities, Constantin Davaras. Noyes Press, 1976.

Essays in Memory of Karl Lehmann, J.L. Caskey. New York, 1964.

Études Crétoises, vol. 1–19. École française d'Athènes. Paris, 1928–74.

Études Déliennes. Bulletin de Correspondance Hellenique, Suppl. 1, 1973.

Études Thasiennes. L'École française d'Athènes. Paris, 1944–.

Excavation in Chios 1952–1955: Greek Emporio, John Boardman. BSA Suppl. no. 6, 1967.

Excavations at Phylakopi in Melos. JHS Suppl. 4, 1904.

Excavations at Saliagos near Antiparos, J.D. Evans and Colin Renfrew. *BSA* Suppl. no. 5, Oxford, 1968.

Excavations at Thera, vols. 1–6. Sp. Marinatos. Athens, 1968–74.

Excavations at Thermi in Lesbos, Winifred Lamb. Cambridge, 1936.

Excavations in Eastern Crete, Vrokastro. E.H. Hall. *Univ. of Penn. Museum Anthropological Publications,* vol. 3, no. 3, 1914.

Excavations on the Island of Pseira, R.B. Seager. *Univ. of Penn. Museum Anthropological Publications,* 1910.

Exploration archéologique de Délos. École française de'Athènes. 1909–.

Explorations on the Island of Mochlos, R.B. Seager. American School of Classical Studies, Boston, 1912.

Faure, *Fonctions des cavernes crétoises.* École française d'Athènes, *Travaux et*
Fonctions *mémories,* fasc. 14. Paris, 1964.

Festschrift P. Goessler, E.M. Bossert. Berlin, 1954.

Fouilles de Vroulia, K.F. Kinch. Berlin, 1914.

Furtwängler, *Aegina, das Heiligtum der Aphaia,* Furtwängler, Thiersch, and Fiechter.
Aegina Munich, 1906.

Gears from the Greeks, D. Price. New York, 1975.

Gournia *Gournia, Vasiliki and Other Sites on the Isthmus of Hierapetra, Crete,* Harriet Boyd-Hawes, B.E. Williams, et al.

Guide de Thasos. École française d'Athènes, 1967.

A Handbook to the Palace of Minos, Knossos, J.D.S. Pendlebury, 1954.

Hysterominoikai Taphai Limenos Knosou, Alexiou. Library of the Archaeological Society, 1967.

IG *Inscriptiones Gracae,* 15 vols. De Gruyter.

L'île de Rhodes, E. Biliotti et l'Abbé Cottret. Rhodes, 1881.

Inglieri *Carta Archeologica dell'Isola de Rodi,* R.U. Inglieri. Fiorenze, 1936.

Die Insel Kythera, R. Leonhard. Gotha, 1899.

Die Insel Leros, L. Bürchner. Munich, 1898.

Die Insel Zakynthos, B. Schmidt, 1899.

Ithaka, der Peloponnes und Troja, Heinrich Schliemann. Leipzig, 1869, reprint Darmstadt, 1963.

Korkyra *Korkyra, archaische Bauten und Bildwerke.* Archäologisches Institut des Deutschens Reiches, Berlin 1939–40. Band I: *Der Artemistempel,* H. Schlief, K. Rhomaios. Band II: *Die Bildwerke,* G. Rodenwalt.

Knossos, The Sanctuary of Demeter, J.N. Coldstream. BSA Suppl. no. 8, London, 1973.

Koische Forschungen und Funde, R. Herzog. Leipzig, 1899.

Kos, Ergebnisse der deutschen Ausgrabungen und Forschungen. Band I: *Asklepieion,* R. Herzog and P. Schazmann. Berlin, 1932.

Kretische Bronzereliefs, E. Kunze. Stuttgart, 1931.

Kythera, J.N. Coldstream, G.L. Huxley, et al. Noyes Press, 1972.

The Last Days of the Palace at Knossos, M.R. Popham. *Studies in Mediterranean Archaeology,* no. 5 Lund, 1964.

Lindos *Lindos, Fouilles et Recherches 1902–1914,* Fondation Carlsberg, Copenhagen. Vol. 1: *Acropolis, Petits Objects.* Berlin, 1931.
Vol. 3: *Le Sanctuaire d'Athana Lindia et l'Architecture Lindienne.* Berlin, 1960.

Matz, For- *Forschungen auf Kreta 1942,* F. Matz, ed. Berlin, 1951.
schungen auf
Kreta

Myrtos, An Early Bronze Age Settlement in Crete, Peter Warren. *BSA* Suppl. no. 7, 1972.

Les Navigations d'Ulysse. Vol. 4: *Nausicaa et le retour d'Ulysse*, Bérard. 1927.

Nécropole de Camiros, Journal des fouilles 1858–1865, A. Salzmann. Paris, 1875.

Nécropoles du Mirabella, H. van Effenterre. *Études Crétoises, vol. 8, Paris, 1948*.

Ovalhaus und Palast in Kreta, Noack. Leipzig, 1928.

*Oxford Classical Dictionary*², N.G.L. Hammond and H.H. Scullard, editors. Oxford, Clarendon Press, 1970.

P. of M.   *The Palace of Minos*, vols. 1–4, Sir Arthur Evans. London, 1921–35.

Pashley,   *Travels in Crete*, R. Pashley, 2 vols. Cambridge, 1832.
Travels

Il Palazzo Minoico de Festos, L. Pernier and L. Banti. Rome, 1935–51.

Poliochni, L. Bernabò-Brea. Rome, 1964.

Prehistoric Tombs of Knossos, Sir Arthur Evans. London, 1906.

The Present State of the Islands, Bernard Randolph. Oxford, 1687.

RE   *Realencyclopädie der classichen Altertumswissenschaft*, Pauly-Wissowa.

The Recent Excavations at Phaistos, D. Levi. *Studies in Mediterranean Architecture*, no. 9. Lund, 1964.

Recherches Archéologiques sur les Iles Ioniennes, Riemann. 1879.

Reise auf den Inseln des Thr. Meeres, A.D.L. Conze. Hannover, 1960.

Reisen   *Reisen auf den griechischen Inseln*, 3 vols., Ludwig Ross. Stuttgart, 1840–45.

Reisen und Untersuchungen in Griechenland, P.O. Bröndsted. Paris, 1826.

Renfrew,   *The Emergence of Civilization*, Colin Renfrew. London, 1972.
Emergence

The Rhodian Peraea and Islands, P.M. Fraser and G.E. Bean. Oxford, 1954.

Samos I: Die prähistorische Siedlung unter dem Heraion, V. Milojcic. Bonn, 1961.

Samothrace, Excavations Conducted by the Institute of Fine Arts of New York University. The Bollinger Foundation, N.Y., 1958–.

Santorin et ses éruptions, Fouqué. Paris, 1879.

Il Santuario sull'Acropoli di Gortina, G. Rizza and V. Scrinari. *Monografie della Scuola Arch. di Atène*. Rome, 1968.

Sphoungaras   *Excavations at Sphoungaras in eastern Crete*. E.H. Hall, *University of Pennsylvania Museum Anthropological Publications*, vol. 3, no. 2.

Spratt,   *Travels and Researches in Crete*, T.A.B. Spratt, 1865.
Travels

Studies in Mediterranean Archaeology. Lund, 1964.

Studies Presented to David M. Robinson, Vol. 1. St. Louis, 1951.

Submycenaean Studies, C.-G. Styrenius. Lund, 1967.

The Temples of Jupiter Panhellenius at Aegina, C.R. Cockerell. London, 1860.

Thera   *Thera, Untersuchungen, Vermessungen und Ausgraben in den Jahren 1895–1902*, 4 vols., F. Hiller von Gärtringen. Berlin, 1899–1909.

Travels and Discoveries in the Levant, C.T. Newton. London, 1865.

Troizen und Kalaureia, G. Welter. Berlin, 1941.

Tylissos   *Les villas minoennes de Tylissos*, J. Hazzidakis. *Études Crétoises* 3, Paris, 1934.

VTM   *The Vaulted Tombs of Mesara*, S. Xanthoudides. Liverpool, 1924.

Les vases pré-helléniques et géometriques; Exploration archéologique de Délos, vol. 15, C. Dugas and C. Rhomaios. 1934.

Zagora I, A. Cambitoglou et al. Sidney University Press, 1971.

Zakros, the Discovery of a Lost Palace at Ancient Crete, N. Platon, 1971.

Zois,   *Provlimata Chronologias tis Minoikis Kerameikis*, A. Zois. Library of the
Problems   Archaeological Society, 1969.

PLACE NAME INDEX

This index includes all place names mentioned in this book. Since these names have been taken from numerous periodicals in many languages, their spellings vary, and no attempt has been made to transliterate any specific name on a consistent basis.